How to Be Your
Own Script Doctor

How to Be Your Own Script Doctor

Jennifer E. Kenning

NEW YORK • LONDON

The Continuum International Publishing Group
80 Maiden Lane, New York, NY 10038

The Continuum International Publishing Group Ltd
The Tower Building, 11 York Road, London SE1 7NX

Cover design: Brenda Klinger

Library of Congress Cataloging-in-Publication Data

Kenning, Jennifer E.
  How to be your own script doctor / Jennifer E. Kenning.
    p. cm.
  ISBN-13: 978-0-8264-1747-3 (pbk.)
1. Motion picture plays—Editing. I. Title.
  PN1996.K39 2006
  808.2'3—dc22

                                                    2005027210

06 07 08 09 10 11   10 9 8 7 6 5 4 3 2 1

For Scott,
whose presence in my life
is more inspirational
than any film could ever be,
no matter how developed the premise,
characters, plot, and dialogue.
I will love you forever . . . and one day.

Contents

Acknowledgments

FOR ALL OF THE TIME, guidance, and support I have received from so many during the writing of this book, I feel it only appropriate to honor them by taking some of my time to say thank you.

To my husband, Scott, who has sacrificed so much to make my dreams come true no matter how crazy they sometimes seemed.

To my mother, Cathy, who taught me that anything is possible and to never, ever settle. I draw strength from her every day as I continue to live as the independent woman she inspired me to be.

To Ken and Janice, whose enthusiasm for the book and confidence in my writing is much appreciated. In addition, I thank them for allowing me to spread out at their place with my laptop, Post-it® notes, disks, pens, reams of paper, and other writing supplies.

To my editor, David Barker—I thank him for believing in this book and in me. Although we communicated heavily through e-mail, he managed to make every message personal—as if we were conversing face-to-face. I will always remember and appreciate the opportunity he gave me to write this book.

To my clients, especially to Mark Kurasz—thank you for allowing me to use wonderful examples of your cinematic brilliance in this book.

To my late grandfather, Bob, whose spirit gives me comfort and illuminates all the times of darkness.

Finally, thank you to Harley for always keeping me company.

Introduction

JAMES CLAVELL ONCE SAID, "The art of writing is rewriting." It doesn't take much to realize how true that statement is. When you finish the first draft of a screenplay, it is far from ready for submission to an agent or studio. The screenplay needs to be analyzed and refined.

But how do you even know what areas need refining? Some seek the opinions of family and friends—only to receive overly biased feedback that offers nothing to improve the script. Others seek the aid of professional story analysts (or doctors)—spending hundreds, even thousands of dollars for their services.

This book is the perfect alternative and solution to the opinions above. It teaches screenwriters the skills to objectively analyze and professionally revise their own scripts without spending a lot of money.

How to Be Your Own Script Doctor is not a book on how to write a screenplay. Instead, it is a comprehensive book for the rewriting process of a screenplay. It therefore assumes that the reader of this book has completed a script. Thus, I frequently refer to my intended audience as *rewriters* instead of *writers*.

Whether novice or experienced, any screenwriter will benefit from the material in this book. Likewise, it will help whether the completed screenplay is original or an adaptation. *How to Be Your Own Script Doctor* is structured and presented in a manner that comprehensively and cohesively explores each aspect of any feature film screenplay.

- Part I teaches or simply refreshes the analytical skills screenrewriters need to assess their screenplays.
- Part II details the specific areas of a screenplay—scene, premise, theme, character, structure, plot, and dialogue. The sections for each area include recognizing symptoms, diagnosing the problem or problems within the specific area, learning more about the problem area, and then treating the diagnosed problem.
- Part III explores what is often neglected but equally important during the assessment and refinement process of a script, marketability and techniques to improve a screenplay's commercial appeal.
- Part IV (like a screenplay) ties up all of the loose ends of the script analysis, including proper formatting, copyediting, and protection from unauthorized use.

The overall approach of *How to Be Your Own Script Doctor* is contemporary. Except for two critical films, I only reference films from 1980 to the present, still allowing examination of a number of tremendously successful films, both at the box office and in the Nielsen ratings. Whereas Luke Skywalker is referenced in several screenwriting books as the classic hero, *How to Be Your Own Script Doctor* references instead the journey of Frodo Baggins—the new age and destined-to-be-classic cinematic hero.

Although my goal in writing *How to Be Your Own Script Doctor* is to teach screenwriters and rewriters objective analysis and professional refinement, I must emphasize that refinement by no means suggests demolishing all that you have created. Refinement simply means polishing what you have created to bring out its true brilliance and value.

PART I

Prepping for Script Surgery

CHAPTER 1

Refreshing Drops
for the Analytical Eye

"Sharp pencils are a good thing to have when you edit. A sharp mind is better."

—Barry Tarshis

A SCREENPLAY, LIKE AN ONION, has many layers. As such, your screenplay is just as likely to make you cry—possibly due to its tragic or hilarious plot line or from the sheer frustration of trudging through its layers. The first may be a good thing and altogether inevitable if the script is doing what it should—that is, evoke emotion. The latter is unnecessary and avoidable. You have a relationship with your script, a bond that has grown between the two of you since birth or FADE IN. Creatively, you wrote the first draft of your screenplay from your heart. Like any relationship, heart and head swap roles like a teeter-totter, back and forth. In the case of a screenplay's rewrite, creative thinking steps back and critical thinking steps forward. Although your first draft may contain all the basic elements of a screenplay, including but in no way limited to an engaging premise and compelling characters, it is like a pearl plucked from an oyster; it must be washed and polished before its true worth and beauty can be recognized.

Fine-tuning your own analytical or critical thinking skills is crucial, because writers always need editing and constructive criticism. And we don't always find the constructive criticism we are looking for from family and friends, who can't help but let their loving biases influence their opinions. So we often look to third-party professionals (such as script doctors) who know how to give constructive analytical feedback on a script, clearly summarizing what the story is about and then making beneficial comments and suggestions for improvement. Unfortunately, such help can be expensive. The great news is that you don't need to seek professional help or ask mom or dad or your spouse or coworker for the constructive criticism you seek. You can be your own script doctor: your skills just need to be honed. As your own script doctor, using your sharpened analytical skills, you will apply logic instead of emotion to the evaluation and rewrite of your script.

When a story analyst reads a script, it is his or her job to keep the writer's intentions and *only* the writer's intentions in mind. When I read scripts submitted to me by my clients, I ask myself: What does the writer have in mind here? What might the writer be thinking? Likewise, you as the rewriter should be asking yourself the same questions during analysis: What do *I* have in mind here? What am *I* thinking? Script doctors, story analysts, and consultants simply analyze—they use their critical thinking skills to examine the script before them and determine what works, what doesn't, and why. This chapter will enable you to develop or simply refresh your own critical thinking skills so that you can examine your own script effectively and professionally.

If you are open to it, you can learn how to think analytically. It may seem impossible, but didn't finishing your screenplay feel impossible at times as well? You must have finished it, because you are reading this book. Nothing is impossible.

Before breaking down and analyzing a screenplay, review of the five guidelines listed below is crucial. I consistently repeat these to myself before analyzing any script—be it my own or a client's.

1. *Have passion.* You must have had passion while writing your script, since you finished the first draft. Now you must carry that passion through to the rewrite. Passion is what will keep

you going when you come face-to-face with some tough analysis and it will show up in the end product.

2. *Be suspicious of everything in the script.* This encourages you to examine all elements in your script. Comprehensiveness is the key—every aspect must be looked at and properly assessed.

3. *Have a good attitude and confidence.* Remember, if you can finish a first draft, you can certainly complete the rewrite. Stay positive. Trust that your analysis of a good story told from the heart will eventually transform it for the better through what comes from your head.

4. *Be open-minded.* Be open to the possibility of other solutions to the problem parts of your story.

5. *Have thick skin.* This guideline doesn't just apply to what you need when submitting your baby and getting rejection after rejection from various agents, producers, and studios. Although I may love certain aspects of a client's script and would like to check "pass" solely based on those aspects, I must keep in mind that if the script is lacking in other important areas, I need to put aside my personal preferences and keep my client's best interests in mind. In your own analysis, you too will need to develop thick skin for the *self*-rejections you will end up doing to your own work. No matter how little experience you may have with analytical thinking or how difficult the critical thinking process may seem and be at times, it has one crucial goal: to improve with your mind what you have written from your heart.

What It Means to Think

Thinking is both a conscious and unconscious (controlled) activity that humans perform mentally in an effort to solve a problem. When you think consciously, solutions rise consistently, but not always as easily as when you think unconsciously about something. How many instances can you think of where solutions to problems just came to you when least expected? How many solutions came when you put the problem aside in an attempt to create space between you and the problem—not "thinking" about it?

The thinking process includes several actions taken by the thinker in order to solve a problem. The actions are rarely, if ever, performed singularly. Instead, they are performed in combination and in no particular order. Actions you may experience during the thinking process include:

- Observing
- Recalling
- Asking (curiosity and suspiciousness)
- Visualizing
- Assessing
- Judging
- Decoding and understanding

What It Means to Think Analytically

For our purpose, analyzing is the process of examining what you have produced (in this case, a script), deciding the best way to solve what doesn't work, and then applying that solution to your satisfaction so that it best enhances the product.

Analyzing a screenplay is an intricate process that is the same for any document—it entails breaking apart the individual elements and relationally subjecting those elements to each other and to the whole. Therefore, analysis of a screenplay can be thought of as the understanding and refinement of the whole script by breaking it down into the parts or elements that comprise it. These elements are scene, premise, theme, structure, plot, character, dialogue, market conditions, and commerciality.

The two phases of analytical thinking (the production phase and the examination phase) intertwine to help us find and apply solutions to problems.

The production phase involves producing solution possibilities for the problems in each of the separate parts of your script. In the production phase of analytical thinking, you call upon all of your talents—independence, resourcefulness, intuition, passion, and dedication—to produce possible solutions to your script problems.

There are several ways to solve problems, but it is in the examination phase that you assess, decipher, and decide which solution is the best. The examination phase assesses the ideas you have produced in the production phase of analytical thinking. The examination phase is a trial-and-error process—you are testing your ideas for solutions by looking for positives and negatives, deciphering which solutions are logically the best, and then applying them.

The ability to assess a literary work such as a screenplay analytically is a powerful thing. Let's put it this way: one of the most important attributes of a résumé is the presence of verbs denoting that you are a dynamic person. If you were to include analytical thinking as a skill on your résumé, that skill would automatically link you to verbs such as resolving, communicating, learning, solving, developing, and broadening. That's one powerful skill.

Analytical or critical thinking is not all inclusive, at least not 100 percent of the time. In other words, you won't detect all of the flaws in your screenplay no matter how thorough your analysis. However, by critically assessing your script, you will significantly reduce the number of errors and problems in it.

Analytical processes such as thinking, reading, and writing only improve with practice. Hence, the more scripts you write and evaluate, the better your analysis of them will be.

The Mysterious Brain and Its Role in Analysis

There are two sides to the human brain—the left hemisphere and the right hemisphere. Each hemisphere has its own distinct role and responsibilities.

From the right hemisphere comes everything we do intuitively and creatively. As a result, when first writing a screenplay, we are able to trust our instincts and write what comes out of our hearts and onto the paper or computer. In contrast, the left hemisphere is responsible for everything we do logically, judgmentally, and analytically. The left hemisphere works sequentially and scientifically.

The two hemispheres of the brain seem comparable to art vs. science. Moreover, art and science seem to be the core of a script. On the one hand, a script is art; on the other, it follows a form—a scientific structure allowing creativity to flow logically.

Despite the fact that the brain has two hemispheres or areas of emphasis, it does not mean that a person uses only one hemisphere from birth (as in left-brained and right-brained people), leaving the other hemisphere dead or just taking up space. In fact, you will make the shift from the creative side of your brain, responsible for the writing of the script, to the other, scientific side, responsible for the refining of your script, with no trouble. As you refine each area of your script, you will continue to toggle between the right hemisphere and the left hemisphere.

Although the human brain loses cells with age, it never stops growing. This is good news, because it means that everyone is capable of learning or sharpening his or her analytical skills. To promote growth and learning, the brain needs to be stimulated and challenged.

You can "warm up your brain" to think analytically by following these proven methods of brain stimulation:

- *Get ample sleep.* Seven-and-a-half to eight-and-a-half hours' sleep if possible. If this is not possible, take brief power naps throughout the day to rest and refresh your brain.
- *Eat nutritious foods.* When your body is well nourished, your brain function will be better. A diet rich in vegetables, fruits, and—particularly—fish helps to maintain a healthy body and aids in brain health. The omega-3 fatty acids found in fish prevent inflammation of the brain cells, helping to maintain the brain's analytical thinking and reasoning processes.

- *Drink water.* Eight to ten glasses of water a day to prevent dehydration, which causes stress and impairs thinking.
- *Engage in aerobic exercise.* The endorphins released during aerobics reduce stress and improve memory. Of course, always consult your doctor before starting any exercise regime.
- *Employ fun and games.* Constructing a jigsaw puzzle or working on a word-find or crossword puzzle have been proven to stimulate and maintain brain activity. I like to play a game of solitaire on my computer before I start working.
- *Listen to music.* Like aerobic exercise, music has been linked to releasing endorphins, therefore reducing stress and improving memory, which, as you already know, improves your overall brain function. There are even music CDs specifically designed for the body and brain, such as the Sonicaid CDs created by Lee R. Bartel, PhD, who is an expert in cognitive thinking and the emotional response humans have to music. Dr. Bartel has created a series of four CDs, including *Music to Inspire Creativity*, *Music to Improve Relaxation*, *Music to Enhance Concentration*, and *Music to Promote Sleep.*
- *Try aromatherapy.* Aromatherapy is popular and analytical thinking is one more situation where you can benefit from certain scents. Although there are many aromas that evoke different reactions, some of the most popular are peppermint, eucalyptus, and lavender. When I ran for my college's track team, I sucked peppermint candies before each race because my coach told me that the smell helped with relaxation, clarity, and focus. Likewise, if I am at home, I light a peppermint candle while I write. If I am writing away from home, I carry lotion containing eucalyptus and mint. Many inexpensive products containing these and other stimulating scents are on the market; it may be worth it for you to try one.

Overcoming Obstacles to Analytical Thinking

As an analytical thinker assessing your own script, you are susceptible to a couple of problems—your familiarity with the product and your ego, both of which can interfere with your ability to assess the script objectively. Analyzing your own ideas can be difficult, but there are ways to overcome the difficulty. It is human nature to be defensive of something that is ours. We have that bond, the connection that tells us it is ours and it couldn't possibly be wrong. We are like parents protecting our baby and incapable of seeing any imperfections.

Completely breaking the self-bias barrier between you and your script is impossible and not even necessary—there should be a balance of objectivity and subjectivity in any good analytical evaluation. The ways we examine ideas and make judgments are heavily influenced by whose ideas we are examining and judging—again, this is human nature. Moreover, you may be predisposed to being easy or tough on your own ideas . . . and that's fine. Just make sure your opinion isn't solely based on the fact that they are *your* ideas.

The first step to overcome excessive self-bias is to acknowledge your biases and prejudices. Subjective thinking clouds the analytical process when it is denied. By acknowledging a bias, you are being honest with yourself and keeping an open mind. Being open to change instead of resisting it aids in overcoming self-bias because you will be able and willing to consider other perspectives. You will also be able to reevaluate your priorities if necessary.

When you are finally open to the notion of exploring other ideas, welcome them, but still subject them to a trial-and-error process. Remember, be suspicious and weigh the new to make sure it fits properly within its context.

Patterns

You will begin to notice while assessing and refining your screenplay that all of the content contained within it is interlinked. David Trottier says it well in *The Screenwriter's Bible*: "[W]hen revising, if solving one problem also solves another problem, you're on the right track." All of the components of a screenplay have the potential to compliment each other. Likewise, all of the components have the potential to damage each other.

Specific patterns and commonalities in all areas of your screenplay will soon become visible to you. These include:

- Dynamic vs. static
- Incremental intensification
- Internal vs. external
- Genre dependence
- Delay

In addition, you will notice interesting juxtapositions in your script, such as (but not limited to) plot and character, dialogue and action, structure and spontaneity.

The most frequent and critical pattern you should notice, however, is cause and effect, stimulus and reaction. These are mandatory for all forms of fiction because fiction requires cause and effect in order to create credibility. Credibility translates into believability—a necessity for the audience to fully engage with your story.

Prepping the O.R.

The proper environment for script surgery will enhance or cripple the procedure. Below are three preps to ensure a pleasant, successful script analysis.

- *Time off.* To overcome self-bias, the writer must take time away from the script once it is written. If possible, I would suggest letting it sit for at least two weeks. If you start the rewrite immediately, your heart will still be too attached to what has been created. Thus, the chasm between creativity and logic will not be easily traversed.
- *Location.* Once you have taken time off, you will come back refreshed. The next step is to decide what time of day you work best and where you work best. You may even discover

that the time and space that works for you in the creative stage differs from the best time and space for your analytical work. I work best between 9:00 p.m. and 3:00 a.m.—creatively and analytically. As for location, I can work just about anywhere—my desk, kitchen table, or coffee table. However, I need to have the stereo, TV, fan, or humidifier on. My need to have some noise while I'm working started back when I was in high school and stuck with me through college and my career. You could say that I am a big fan of white noise . . . no pun intended. But every rewriter is different. You need to find what works best for you. Lighting is also crucial. Make sure the area where you are conducting your analysis is well lit.

- *Supplies.* Now that you know when and where you work best, you must prepare your surroundings for whatever might come at you. I like to keep a voice recorder or a mini notebook with me. I also stock up on pencils and red pens. For electronic scripts that clients send to me, I sometimes turn the tracking on and go through the script that way. However, I prefer to have a hard copy in hand when I do analysis on a script (or on any writing, for that matter). Whatever your preference, it may be helpful for you to change your method every now and then. Change allows you to view things from a different perspective and you'll see things you might otherwise miss.

If you come to a snag in the script that you just cannot figure out, leave it and come back to it. The more time you spend stuck on it will only cause you unnecessary stress and frustration, which can restrict brain stimulation, growth, and learning. Think back to standardized testing, how the administrators always advised you to skip and return to difficult question(s). The same concept and advice applies here.

Remember, although it may be frustrating and painful, your main objective in analyzing your script is to make it better in all aspects—objectively, thematically, mechanically, and commercially.

Your Surgical Schedule

Following a clear, logical order for your script analysis will help keep you organized and efficient. Since each script demands different amounts of attention to the various areas, the following list is meant as a guideline, not a strict, rigid rule. Areas of emphasis for your analysis include:

- Scene
- Premise
- Theme
- Character
- Structure and plot
- Dialogue
- Market/commercial potential
- Copyediting

Although you may need to spend more time on one area than on another, you will still need to:

- *Prioritize.* The best scripts are those that incorporate all of the previously mentioned parts of a script. However, every buyer is looking for a solid story and characters, so always put the most emphasis on them.
- *Ask questions.* Ask questions of each area of the script and of yourself. Know your intentions. As the author, ask yourself, "What was I intending for X?"
- *Be specific.* Write down the details and be specific with your comments and criticisms.

Sometimes I do basic editing on my clients' scripts, including correcting typos and grammatical errors. Occasionally, a client asks me to do a final proofreading. Although I would suggest waiting to do this type of editing until you have completed your analysis and rewrite, I cannot stress enough the importance of not skipping this step. Minor grammatical and typographical errors will definitely have a negative effect on whoever reads your completed script and will immediately mark you as an amateur. Once you yourself have done the analysis and copyediting, find someone else to do a final proofreading. This one minor rewriting process step has a major impact.

Now that you have learned or refreshed your analytical skills, it's time to start applying them.

CHAPTER 2

Scalpel!

"To find out what doesn't work is an important step toward determining what does."

—Vincent Ryan Ruggiero

WHEN YOU GO TO A PHYSICIAN, the doctor talks to you and assesses your symptoms before conducting the actual physical examination. The physician does this in order to accurately and logically diagnose your problem. The doctor discovers the symptoms by asking many questions.

Before you begin the thorough examination of your script, acting as your own script doctor so you can diagnose the problem and treat it, you need to uncover the symptoms. To diagnose your script's problems, you will ask questions of your script—a lot of questions. As Vincent Ryan Ruggiero states in *The Art of Thinking: A Guide to Critical and Creative Thought*, "The people who make breakthroughs and achieve insights are those who wonder. And their wondering extends to the causes of things: how they got to be the way they are and how they work." You are asking questions of your script so that later you can determine if the choices you made derive from the proper cause—making sure that through the relationships of your script's parts, the entire story flows logically. You are reasoning and, in fact, logic is the study of reasoning.

The more ideas you can produce from the questions you ask, the better. The way to evaluate anything is to ask questions. In their book, *Writing Analytically*, Jill Stephen and David Rosenwasser state, "Learning to write well is largely a matter of learning how to frame questions." The following chapters of the book will guide you through the examination of your screenplay *after* you have asked and answered a detailed list of questions.

This chapter contains over two hundred questions for you to ask of yourself and your script to help you find the areas in need of refinement. If you are unfamiliar with any of the terminology, see the glossary on page 157. You may discover that every part of the script needs attention, or you may find that only certain sections need help. In any case, the comprehensiveness of these questions guarantees that you will cover all the bases of your script. I have listed them by scene, premise, theme, character, structure, plot, dialogue, and marketability. The questions themselves—and the order of this book's chapters—are arranged in the order that a professional script doctor would conduct his or her analysis. Some of the questions are very similar to each other. In addition, some questions may seem as if they are out of sequence. This is intentionally to prevent anticipation of the next question. The questions as they appear make you think deeply about your answers and help you avoid contrived and trite answers. Now, let's begin asking questions about the individual areas of your script.

Scenes

The following questions will help you assess potential scene problems in your script. Chapter 3 covers scenes and how to refine them. Ask yourself:

- Do my scenes have a justifiable reason for being in the script?
- Do my scenes move the story forward, all building toward the climax of the script?

- Does each scene start at the latest possible moment that it can, omitting all other information that isn't relevant or necessary to the story?
- Are my scenes entertaining?
- Are the scenes visual enough? Do they show instead of tell?
- Does each scene end at the earliest possible point that it can?
- Is the scene boring?
- Do I have scenes that are repetitive?
- What is the point of the scene?
- Why include this scene?
- What is the most important information or point the audience needs to understand and take from this scene?
- What is the scene's direction?
- What is the focus of the scene?
- Is the viewpoint of the scene clear?
- Whose scene is it?
- Is the objective of the scene clear?
- What is the conflict of the scene? Is it external? Internal?
- Where does the scene take place?
- Are there too many characters in the scene?
- Does the goal of the scene somehow coincide with the overall story goal?
- Do all of the props in the scene serve a purpose?
- Does the scene contain as few directing elements as possible, such as camera angles, transitional devices, etc.?
- Does each scene transition itself into the next, therefore continuously moving the story forward?
- Do the obstacles of the scene match the intensity of the scene? Are they difficult enough? Too difficult?
- Is there any character revelation in the scene?
- In the beginning of the scene, what is at stake for the character?
- What is at stake at the end of the scene for the character?
- How many characters enter, remain, and exit the scene at any given time?

- When does the scene take place?
- Does the scene have an ending?
- Does the scene ending create anticipation for the next scene?
- How long are my scenes?
- Are any new characters introduced in the scenes?
- Are any transitional devices used before or after the scene?
- Does the scene parallel the whole story in terms of theme?
- Does the scene foreshadow events and situations to come?
- Does the scene contrast with the scene preceding it?
- Does the scene contrast with the scene that follows it?
- Is there dramatic irony in the scene?
- Is the first scene of the script visually stunning and does it provide a natural transition into the problem of the protagonist that sets him or her on the journey?

Premise and Theme

The following questions will help you assess potential premise and theme problems in your script. Chapter 4 will cover premise and theme, and how to refine both of them. Ask yourself:

- Is the premise creative?
- Is the premise commercial?
- Is the premise original?
- Will the premise appeal to a mass audience?
- Is the premise intriguing?
- Does the premise create a real sense of yearning to read the entire script?
- Can the premise be understood from the title given to the script?
- Is the theme strong?
- Does the theme go beyond entertainment value? Does it express a moral?
- Does the theme have mass audience appeal, or is it restricted to a particular demographic?
- Is the theme overbearing?
- Is the theme condescending?

- What am I and my characters trying to say through the story? In other words, what is the message of the story?
- Is the theme acknowledged at the resolution point of the story?
- Is the theme too preachy?
- Have I forced the theme or let it come naturally through the flow of the story?

Character

The following questions will help you assess potential character problems in your script. Chapter 5 covers characters and how to refine them. Ask yourself:

- Does my character(s) grow?
- How does my character(s) grow?
- Can I show how my character(s) grows?
- What does my protagonist want?
- What does my antagonist need?
- Do both my protagonist and antagonist have a strong enough desire for whatever it is they want?
- How do my characters handle pressure and obstacles?
- What are my characters' personalities?
- What does my protagonist need?
- How do my characters perceive themselves?
- How do I perceive my characters?
- How are my characters challenged internally?
- What is the purpose of each character in the script?
- Is there a relatable character flaw within the main character?
- What does my antagonist want?
- Is my protagonist sympathetic?
- Are there any moments of self-realization for my characters—for my protagonist, especially?
- Are the supporting characters fully developed?
- Are the relationships between the characters completely developed?

- How are my characters challenged externally?
- Are the characters three-dimensional, or are they flat and boring?
- Are the characters believable?
- Are the characters stereotypical?
- Why does my main character want what he or she wants? In other words, what is driving the main character to achieve his or her goal?
- Is the antagonist sympathetic?
- Who or what is trying to prevent my main character from achieving his or her goal?
- What is my character's motivation for achieving the goal?
- Does my protagonist have an aspect of his or her life where there is room to grow—emotionally, spiritually, etc.?
- How does my main character view life? Others? Self?
- What are my characters' (particularly my protagonist's) unique psychological, physical, and sociological qualities?
- What are the back-stories of my characters, particularly of my protagonist?
- Does my protagonist have any distinct character flaws?
- Would the role of my antagonist be appealing to a star actor/actress?
- Is the protagonist someone the audience will relate to?
- Is the antagonist strong and powerful?
- How is my protagonist different at the end of the story compared to the beginning?
- Has my protagonist learned anything new that he or she didn't know at the beginning of the story?
- How does my main character view others?
- Is my protagonist someone the audience will like?
- Would the role of my protagonist be appealing to a star actor/actress?
- Are the characters original, or are they prototypes of similar characters?
- Is the antagonist stronger and more powerful than the protagonist?
- How does my main character view him- or herself?

Structure and Plot

The following questions will help you assess potential structure and plot problems in your script. Chapter 6 discusses structure and plot, and how to refine both of them. Ask yourself:

- Is the story written in a distinct three-act structure?
- Does the first act set up the rest of the story?
- Does the script contain enough obstacles and conflict in the second act to sustain the audience's participation and interest?
- Does the story start at the latest possible point that it can?
- Does the first act employ a hook within the first ten pages of the script?
- How is the hook employed? Visually? In the narrative?
- Does the third act tie up all the loose ends of the story?
- Does the first act properly set up the conflict for the rest of the story?
- Is the story question clear?
- Does each of the turning points reaffirm the story question?
- Is the inciting incident clear?
- Does the first turning point lead the character and audience into the second act?
- Does the second act develop the characters, relationships, and subplots through the employment of obstacles and conflict?
- Is the climax as intense as it possibly can and should be?
- Do the subplots bring dimension to the main storyline?
- Does the second turning point lead the character and audience into the third act?
- Are all of the subplots necessary?
- Does each individual subplot have structure, with its own distinct beginning, middle, and end?
- Are there too few subplots?
- How is the main conflict introduced? How is it resolved?
- Are the setting and location unique?
- Is there a unique voice and tone to my story?

- Is the story believable within the genre I have chosen?
- Do the subplots parallel the main story plot?
- Does the second act develop the premise?
- Is the transition between scenes seamless?
- Does the story unfold in a way that makes it unpredictable?
- What is the pace of the story?
- Are there both light-hearted and heavy-hearted scenes?
- Do the climax and resolution of the subplot(s) coincide with the plot of the main story?
- Through dialogue and action, does the story build incrementally in intensity towards the climax?
- Does the pace reflect the ambience and theme of the story?
- Are there too many beats in the story?
- Is there a sense of urgency or a "ticking clock" in the second act?
- Where does the story take place?
- What is the tone of the story?
- Would the story work better if set in a different time and place?
- What is the inciting incident or catalyst that happens to the main character in act one?
- When does the story take place?
- Does the conflict in act two become stronger and rise throughout the act?
- Is there a reaffirmation of the goal halfway through the story (commonly referred to as the midpoint)?
- What happens in the beginning of the story that disrupts my character's normal life and pushes the story into motion?
- Does the low point heighten anticipation and anxiety for the audience?
- What is the climax in the plot?
- Are there too many subplots?
- What is the low point or crisis for my main character?
- How is the story resolved?
- Is the goal achieved?
- Is the conflict clearly defined?
- Does the story evoke some sort of emotion?

- Can I determine what makes my story unique and original? What is it?
- Does the conflict match the intensity of the story?
- Is the resolution of my story inevitable but not predictable?
- Based on the realm of the story world, is the story believable?
- What happens to the lives of my characters after the goal has or hasn't been achieved?
- Are my plot points (or story points) properly placed within the three-act structure?
- Does my subplot interweave with plot of the main story?
- Is the plot too complex, potentially confusing the audience?

Dialogue

The following questions will help you assess potential dialogue problems in your script. Chapter 7 discusses dialogue and how to refine it. Ask yourself:

- Could the dialogue within the scene be replaced with a look, gesture, or action?
- Does the dialogue sound the way people actually converse?
- In order to reveal what they want, do the characters need to verbalize it?
- Is the dialogue age-sensitive?
- Is there an excessive amount of slang used in the script?
- Does the dialogue match the characteristics, characterization, and background of the character(s)?
- Is the dialogue appropriate for the time period and the setting?
- Do the characters all have distinctive voices, or do they all sound alike?
- Are there excessively long, rambling instances of dialogue?
- Is the dialogue rich or flat?
- Does the dialogue flow smoothly?
- Does the dialogue increase the intensity between characters?
- Is the dialogue too revealing? Not revealing enough?

- Is the dialogue contrived?
- Is the dialogue as lean as possible?
- Does the dialogue contain any subtext?
- How have I revealed exposition?
- Does the dialogue reflect the character who is speaking it, revealing the true persona of the character?
- Do my characters speak with any specific vocabulary, slang, or rhythm?
- Am I showing instead of telling the story?
- Have I revealed too much information too soon to the audience?
- Do my dream sequences and flashbacks serve a purpose? If so, what purpose do they serve?

Marketability

The following questions will help you assess potential marketability problems in your script. Chapters 8 and 9 discuss marketability issues and how to refine your script to better suit the needs and wants of the screenplay marketplace. Ask yourself:

- Does the story appeal to an intended audience?
- Would the script appeal to a superstar actor/actress? Producer? Director?
- Who in the industry is currently buying this genre and style of script?
- Is the story big enough to reach a massive audience, possibly in the millions?
- Can this screenplay be a successful movie?
- Does the screenplay need a celebrity?
- Who has been known in the industry to buy this type of script in the past?
- What is the estimated budget for this script to become a movie?
- What are the best elements of this script?
- Does the script have a catchy, commercial title that would look good on a poster or billboard?

- What does my screenplay still need to be green-lighted into production?
- What is the genre of the script?
- How will an audience react to the story?
- Are any special effects needed to enhance my screenplay?
- Does the projected budget for the script match the budget ordinarily set by the market to which I will be submitting it?
- Will the story reach the intended audience?

Copyediting

The following questions will help you assess any copyediting and post-rewrite areas of the script. Chapter 10 discusses copyediting and all that it entails. Ask yourself:

- Is my script properly formatted?
- Have I registered my script with the Writer's Guild of America and/or the U.S. Copyright Office?
- Is my script free of typos?
- Is my script free of grammatical errors that aren't necessary for the character and/or the story.

PART II

The Scriptectomy

CHAPTER 3

Operation Scene

". . . the more ways you try to rewrite scenes, the more likely you are to develop an integrity about what works and what does not . . ."

—Skip Press

Symptoms of Scene Problems

- Deficient viewpoint
- Loss of scene goal or objective
- Stakes are not high enough
- Lack of forward movement
- Too many people in the scene

WHEN SCENES ARE PROPERLY DEVELOPED, their purposes within a script are uncompromisable. Well-developed scenes move the story forward. In addition, well-developed scenes provide the reader with insights into the characters—feeding and building off the premise and theme of the story.

Scenes have a variety of purposes. They include: introducing a new character, furthering the exposition, providing for quick time passage (as with a montage or a series of short shots used to indicate that time is passing quickly while imparting vital information to the audience with little or no dialogue), foreshadowing events to come, creating dramatic irony, and orienting the audience. Other scenes provide back-story or delineate internal conflict, define the theme, or show pure action. Action scenes tend to hold their own, not needing to fulfill any other purpose, unlike scenes with less intensity, which tend to accomplish more than one function. While a particular scene can have one specific purpose or many purposes, it must always move the story forward.

Scenes are crucial to the success of your screenplay—it's that cause-and-effect relationship we discussed. Accordingly, when you revise or cut your scenes, you should keep in mind the whole script, not just the individual scene. You are looking for the scenes that belong in the story you are attempting to tell and sell.

Scene Structure, Content, and Placement

We could compare the three-act structure of a screenplay to a human skeleton. Like a skeleton, the three-act structure is the framework for all that goes into making a screenplay whole. The scenes of a screenplay are like the bones that make up the skeleton—they are the building blocks of the story.

Scenes that are entirely external are active—they show, not tell. Similarly, they are based on cause and effect, building into sequences and creating unification of story. When scenes are placed in a particular order within the script, the plot and structure begin to take shape. A scene should always cause another scene. In other words, one scene should be the stimulus for the other—this is how the aspects of the story grow and develop, including characters, subplots, action, conflict, and obstacles. If one scene does not flow from the previous scene, your plot will seem contrived.

A scene, an external unit of action, has, like the three-act structure of an entire screenplay, a beginning, a middle, and an end. Within that structure, the scene must contain a viewpoint character, an objective (goal), conflict, and an ending (resolution)—which usually leaves the scene's character further away from his or her scene goal, but closer to the story goal.

At some point, your scenes will need to reveal your characters' traits and behaviors so that their later actions in the story seem logical and acceptable to the audience—a foreshadowing technique. Include such scenes in your script only if the revelations are important and necessary to the progression of the story. In addition, don't reveal something to the audience unless it foreshadows events to come in the story or serves a specific function. This way, you avoid the risk of confusing your audience.

Make sure you include at least two characters in your scenes to ensure dramatic effect and scene evolution and progression. When refining scenes, it is important to decide who belongs and who doesn't based on what each character adds to or subtracts from what is going on in the scene.

Viewpoint

Viewpoint is a technique or aspect of a script that can be very difficult to understand. Simply put, the rewriter chooses a character, not necessarily the protagonist, from the story, and then writes the story from that character's point of view. In a sense, the audience takes on the role of the viewpoint character—knowing, seeing, and hearing only what the viewpoint character knows, sees, and hears.

Other choices of viewpoint beyond single character viewpoint include the omniscient viewpoint (or total knowledge of what's going on with everyone in the story) and the multiple viewpoint (which allows the characters along with the audience to know, view, and hear the same things).

The latter two of the three methods are more difficult to write and are not as popular or effective as the single character viewpoint. Using the single character viewpoint encourages the audience to sympathize and identify with the viewpoint character—and the more focused the screenplay is on the viewpoint character, the more the audience will become involved with the story. Moving the viewpoint from character to character confuses the audience and creates apathy.

Every scene that you write must relate to the viewpoint that you have chosen. For each scene, the rewriter must determine whose scene it is. As David Howard and Edward Mabley state in their book *Tools of Screenwriting: A Writer's Guide to the Craft and Elements of a Screenplay*, "Whose want (or pursuit of an objective) makes a given scene happen?" The viewpoint character chosen for the scene will provide the scene's focus.

Scenes start with the viewpoint character that the scene's objective serves. Be sure that the viewpoint character clearly states and maintains the scene's objective—this helps the audience understand the scene, sympathize with the character, and keeps the scene objective clear. There may be anticipated difficulty for the viewpoint character within the scene, but for the most part, the objective should seem completely attainable by and for the character.

Just as there is a story question always hovering over an entire screenplay based on its premise, a scene is no exception—it too contains an overriding question based on its objective. It is crucial that the scene goal is relevant to the overall story question; otherwise, it breaks the cause-and-effect relationship and your audience will not anticipate the following scene, as they should. For instance, the overall story premise for *Sweet Home Alabama* may read something like this: An up-and-coming New York City fashion designer becomes engaged to the charismatic mayor's son, but must first return to her hometown in Alabama to get divorce papers signed by her estranged husband, all to realize she still has feelings for him. From this, you can draw up the overall story question: Will she marry the mayor's son or stay with her husband?

Now, applying the guidelines above, the scene in which Reese Witherspoon's character (Melanie) first arrives at her husband's house is Melanie's scene—it's written from her point of view and her ultimate objective (or goal) in the scene is to get the divorce papers signed right away and out of the way. She believes she will easily attain her goal. We can conclude that the hovering *scene* question is: Will Melanie get the divorce papers signed? You, the rewriter, must know that her husband will not sign the papers, because if the goal were easily attained, the story would end there.

Entering and Exiting a Scene

When evaluating your scenes, you're probably thinking, "Well, I know what a scene consists of, now how many scenes should I have in my screenplay?" Here's a typical rule of thumb: one typed page in your script equals approximately one minute of screen time. Although different fictional genres have different numbers of scenes, usually screenplays contain between forty and sixty scenes. Most scenes are usually between two and four minutes long—never exceeding four minutes. To achieve that two-to-four-minute range, you must start the scene at the latest possible moment, just as the overall story plot must begin at the latest possible moment. You may find that your scenes have all of the necessary components but give information at the start that is not necessary. You should only present information that will help orient the audience to what's going on and what's about to happen. When the scene ends, the audience should be anticipating what is going to happen next. Jim Levi, a professor in my very first screenwriting course at St. Cloud State University, gave me some great advice about scene length: "Get in, get out, don't linger."

In determining the best spot to start a scene, you must figure out what information the audience needs to know to understand what's going on—this is (in retrospect) the first act of the scene. In the retrospective act two, the conflict and actions develop—making the scene dramatic. Thus, to prevent the scene and script from ending, the scene needs conflict. Audiences love conflict. As much as many audience members avoid conflict in reality, it is what keeps them interested and prevents them from choking on their popcorn after dozing during the film. Conflict is what keeps the audience guessing in each scene. Remember, although *you* know that the character won't reach his or her goal, the audience doesn't or shouldn't—they should just know that he or she hasn't reached it *yet*. Many scenes fail because the stakes aren't high enough. The conflict within a scene is solely the effect of the scene's objective, the cause. Earlier I mentioned that a scene is completely external, meaning it's physically happening before us. Thus, the conflict must be with the viewpoint character and another character or characters, so long as the scene isn't crowded with people, therefore confusing the audience and blurring the objective.

To progress toward the story's end, a scene must end and it must end badly. You are building toward the story climax, piecing your skeleton together bone by bone. As such, your character(s) must keep encountering setbacks. No matter how you manage it, the ending of a scene must be negative, whether bluntly negative or bittersweet with a plentiful load of stipulations. In certain circumstances and scripts, the latter can be more interesting and imaginative, since it creates a moral dilemma for the character.

Memphis Raines in *Gone in Sixty Seconds* is faced with a moral dilemma. After Memphis's kid brother gets in trouble and Raymond Calitri threatens to kill him, Memphis pays a visit to Calitri and pleas for his brother's mercy. The scene question here is: Will Calitri spare Memphis's brother? The answer is a no (negative) . . . unless Memphis can boost fifty cars in twelve hours (stipulation). Seven years earlier, Memphis gave up the life of being the world's greatest car booster to set a good example for his brother (moral dilemma).

No matter if the answer to the scene question is a blunt no or a no with stipulations, at the end, the scene question you must answer is the one you proposed in the beginning of the scene—just as you will be answering the story question at the end of the script. Scenes should expand information about the story question, but should not resolve it. A scene's ending leaves the viewpoint character seemingly worse off than he or she was when entering the scene, but brings the screenplay closer to the story goal. With each developed scene ending, the pressure should significantly increase, implanting character doubts that the goal will be attained. It's pure irony—the viewpoint character appears to be moving backward, but actually is moving forward—like sitting in a train seat facing the opposite direction of where the train is going.

Treatment for Problem Scenes

Cutting is the most effective treatment for the refinement of scenes, and this is why: if one item of the character, goal, conflict, and resolution combination is flawed or missing altogether from a scene, it is an indication that the scene is not necessary. Or, to put it this way, if you can cut the scene without deleting pertinent story beats or without disrupting the flow and coherency of the scenes before and after the cut scene, there is no need to keep the scene in the script. We will discuss finding holes in the plot resulting from cutting scenes in chapter 6.

Cutting out material is one of the most difficult tasks for most writers, but it must be done. I was once told by a professor at UCLA that a great writer is defined by his or her use of the computer's DELETE key. With all of my heart and head (creatively and logically), I believe this. Cutting material out of your work not only proves your knowledge of what makes a good screenplay, but marks you as a professional who is willing to put your ego aside for the betterment of the script—in effect, you are putting your audience's needs before your own. There is no doubt that you will be cutting items out of your script throughout the rewrite. However, cutting scenes is one of the biggest alterations you will make to your script, and it can cause a lot of anxiety. Because screenplay stories are told through scenes, if the screenwriter is incapable of refining or deleting ineffective scenes, there is no reasonable explanation for continuing to write the script. You may have a wonderful concept, but if you can't believably tell the story, you will lose your audience mentally and physically out of the theater. A note to all of you who aren't prepared to circular file your deleted scenes: create a file of all of the scenes you edited out—not only will this keep them close to your heart, but they may come in handy for a future script or later as you work on the current one.

In your first draft, you have probably written hundreds of scenes. Now you should shoot for between forty and sixty scenes in your rewrite and final draft. I've heard many different theories on whether a writer should refine all the scenes he or she has created first and cut later, or vice versa. Here's *my* theory. Cutting scenes, especially the quantity that you need to reach the target number, can be very overwhelming. Why waste your time and energy refining all of the scenes only to later cut a large percentage of them? Here's where your scene edit file comes in handy. After you have cut what blatantly seems unnecessary based on the information you have learned thus far, put the scenes in the file and then refine what you have left over. If something is missing after the editing or if there is a void in the plot, look at your file and see if any of the scenes you previously cut are the missing pieces to the puzzle. Once you have your forty to sixty scenes, assess the scenes once more using the scene-probing questions from chapter 2.

If I show you some successes from already produced scripts that went through the cutting process, you may feel more confident about editing your own script. Here are some scenes from *Star Wars: Episode II - Attack of the Clones* that ended up on the cutting-room floor for the betterment of the script. I chose this film to show that even the "God" of sci-fi, CGI, and filmmaking in general (George Lucas), has to suck it up and get rid of what isn't working to make a brilliant film. Although these scenes were not cut directly from the script (they were shot first), they were removed from the final product in the same way they would be cut from a script. Some of these scenes were Lucas's favorites, but he knew that he needed to overcome his personal fondness for the scenes for the betterment of the film. He needed to edit the scenes that repeated information and weakened the story instead of strengthening it. When it came down to it, he needed to keep relevant scenes and cut those that were irrelevant. A stickler for film length, Lucas was conscious and hard-nosed about cutting the scenes that lengthened the movie unnecessarily. Here are some deleted scenes from *Star Wars: Episode Two - Attack of the Clones*:

- *The scene*: Padmé addresses the senate immediately when the film starts. She pleas and debates for the non-formation of a Republican army. *Why it was cut*: Relating to our discussion about the entering point of a scene, this scene took too long to get moving—Lucas wanted to get into the story faster and found that he could achieve this in a quicker way. He also wanted to shift the scene's objective toward Padmé and her danger rather than linger on the political issues the scene displayed.

- *The scene*: Padmé and Anakin visit her parents' house. The scene depicted good back-story of Padmé (avoidance and denial of such topics as love and politics) and an intimate tension between her and Anakin. *Why it was cut*: Lucas cut the scene because the same ideas and concepts were conveyed in other scenes. By connecting the scene before and after this one, the pace of the plot was quickened—it skipped to the next important plot point for the audience.

- *The scene*: Padmé and Anakin are talking in Padmé's bedroom. *Why it was cut*: Again, it is more back-story on Padmé—her history, passion, and humanity. The information conveyed was just not necessary to the story. There is one very interesting tidbit in this scene—Lucas placed five photos on Padmé's bedroom wall in an effort to show her back-story. According to Lucas, the scene in Padmé's bedroom explored the thematic point of "those that can't adapt, die." Although the scene connected with the story theme, it still needed to be cut, because it was unnecessary to the story. Although the scene wasn't used, this is an excellent example of the effective use of props to help further the story. Note, when it comes to props, don't place them in a scene unless they serve a purpose.

- *The scene*: Dooku interrogates and threatens Padmé after she and Anakin are captured at the droid factory. *Why it was cut*: The scene was cut because it ultimately interrupted the pace of the story and what was most important to the audience (the hovering scene question): will Anakin and Padmé find Obi-Wan and free him? This scene was actually revised and left in the movie—only this time, Dooku interrogates and threatens Obi-Wan instead.

Practice makes perfect. The more you practice writing and rewriting scenes, the easier it will be to recognize and cut what doesn't work and what isn't necessary. In addition, this practice will serve as a dose of Prozac® for all of the anxiety that seems to come with obliterating your own creations.

CHAPTER 4

Operation Premise and Theme

"Hold tightly to your original idea so that your script will maintain balance and integrity of purpose."
—Virginia Oakley

Symptoms of Problem Premises

- Story idea confusion
- Idea not original
- Cannot be explained easily
- Lackluster instead of blockbuster—no commercial appeal

PREMISE AND THEME GO TOGETHER—again, cause and effect. The screenwriter usually first develops these and should refine them first as well. This is because, simply put, premise and theme comprise what your story is about, systematically and theoretically. Concept, thesis, objective, main idea, goal—these are all words that mean exactly the same thing . . . premise. You may remember from chapter 3 that scenes have a master premise or, as I called it, an objective. For clarity and to distinguish between a scene's goal and that of an entire screenplay, I will use the word "objective" for scenes. For the entire script story, I will use "premise," also synonymous and often interchanged with "concept." Both terms mean the same thing. The theme, which I will discuss shortly, is what your story is about morally. Premise causes theme;

without a story idea, there wouldn't be a story moral. That's why premise is executed immediately within the script and the theme comes out at the climax. In *The Art of Dramatic Writing*, Lajos Egri states, "a premise is a basis of argument, something proposed that will lead to a logical conclusion." Although Egri's perception of premise is logical and sounds simple, many things can happen to cause a premise to go awry. You must clearly know what your premise is so that your character is allowed to come alive to proclaim that premise. It is important to have a clear premise and theme, because often the script is bought for the premise alone. In addition, script premises must also have some degree of commercial appeal (the degree of commercial appeal depends on the market, which will be discussed in chapter 9).

Since all elements of the script are based on an idea— characters, plot, dialogue, everything, it is important to go back to the very beginning (the concept) to make sure that what you have developed is born from a clear, precise, creative, and commercial idea. Then the entire story and plot will be clear, precise, creative, cohesive, commercial, and, most importantly, unified.

A good premise requires a combination of creative and commercial capability. Creative capability is very subjective— different people interpret it in different ways. Although there may be some industry norms or preconceived notions pertaining to the creative aspects and capability of a script, there are no hard-nosed rules as to what is right or wrong. Commercial capability is the opposite—it is objective; the numbers don't lie. The film is either a success or it isn't at the box office. Commercial capability is based on facts rather than on opinion. No matter the differences between the two, there remains one similarity— both appeal to the buyers of the script and the audience. Let's look at these more closely, starting with creative capability.

Creative Aspects and Capability of Premise

Creatively, a clear and precise premise will produce a script with well-developed, three-dimensional characters who know exactly what they are after (the goal) and why they are after it (the motivation). Moreover, a clear and precise premise will produce a plot rich in conflict and obstacles for characters to overcome while they are trying to achieve a goal. And it will aid in the definition of your story's overall theme—a universal truth pertaining to life and humanity.

Commercial Aspects and Capability of Premise

A premise with good commercial aspects and capability will produce a story that easily appeals to the people who get screenplays made into feature films. This is because these people, the buyers, are paid to know that the film will appeal to a mass audience— causing them to make a profit on it despite what it cost to produce and market it. The people who get a script made into a movie include studio executives, investors, producers, directors, actors/actresses, and agents and managers.

With the premise, conflict and character information is very apparent. The story premise answers journalistically who, what, when, where, why, and how for your script. The premise is what your story is about—the central conflict of the story. Adam Sandler movies have clear and well-developed premises that make them easy to set up and to see the conflicts that will arise out of them. For example, *Billy Madison* is about an adult returning to grades 1–12 in order to prove himself worthy and capable of running the family business. You can visualize immediately the potential conflicts to come.

There are two main types of premises, high concept and low concept. In order to better understand and explain your premise, you should figure out what type of concept your script represents. Here are the basic descriptions.

High concept is a very simplistic and blatant idea. At the same time, high concept is very aggressive, gimmicky, and commercial. High-concept stories are easy to describe in very few words and often sell well because they instantly appeal to the meager attention span of today's film industry professionals. For instance, an introverted teenager is bitten by a spider and transformed into a crime-fighting spider-man (*Spider-Man*). Almost all high-concept stories such as *Spider-Man* are big-budget Hollywood block-busters. It is as if you can instantly imagine the billboards and movie posters for the film. Independent films tend to focus on the next type of premise, low concept.

Low concepts deal with more complicated subjects. Because low concepts tend to be very deep, structurally and morally, they are tricky to describe and promote effectively compared to high concept. For instance, *The Terminator* (a cyborg from the future is sent to destroy life) is easier to abridge and promote than, say, *Life as a House* (a recently divorced man who lives in a shack gets fired and then discovers he's dying of cancer; to bond with his estranged son, he decides to build a house with him).

High and low concepts are very broad. Within them, there are sub-premises that act as pre-designed or template concepts. The more popular of these templates include fish-out-of-water and coming-of-age.

- Fish-out-of-water concepts take protagonists out of their normal environments and displace them in unfamiliar sur-roundings in order to observe how they react and grow. *Billy Madison* could be placed in the fish-out-of-water cate-gory. Billy is removed from the comforts of a pampered and dependent life and thrust into in an environment where he must fend for himself.
- Coming-of-age or rite-of-passage concepts take protago-nists on a journey from youth to maturity—a developmen-tal process. You could argue that *Billy Madison* is also a coming-of-age concept, since Billy (at the start of the script) is a blatantly immature, spoiled child. Billy grows through-out the story until he becomes a competent adult by the end.
- Angel in disguise or traveling angel, as it is often called, is a concept about a problem solver—a perfect character solves the problems of the other character(s) (for example, *One Magic Christmas, Powder,* and *Michael*).
- The deliverance concept takes the protagonist on a journey of redemption—a character arc that starts out bad and ends

good. Anakin Skywalker is a good example of a protagonist who embarks on a journey of redemption. Anakin actually has an interesting character arc in which he starts out good (*Episodes I* and *II*), turns bad (*Episodes III, IV, V*, and part of *VI*), and is delivered back to good (*Episode VI*).

- The penalizing concept has the seemingly good protagonist in the beginning undergo a character arc that turns him or her bad and he or she is punished at the end. Examples of this concept are *Wall Street* and *Shattered Glass*.

Often these template premises are categorized as genres. This categorization is not an entirely correct practice, because concepts can be found in any genre, but genres cannot be found in concepts. They may be associated with concepts, but not found in them. So concepts are interchangeable; genres are not. Moreover, any premise can sell as long as it contains enough creative and commercial capability. But, not every genre can sell (which we will discuss further in chapter 8).

Some people suggest that you should assess your premise in terms of the medium for which it would be best suited. Does your premise sound like it would work better as a feature-length film, made-for-TV movie, or short film, for instance? A great, well-developed premise will work in any medium. It is the plot development and execution from a particular premise that may make it more suitable for one medium over another.

Again, the least you need to know is that some genres have typically worked better in certain mediums, but a well-executed premise will work in any. Sometimes the premise follows suit of the genre. In one of my early screenwriting courses, within the first week of class I submitted a premise for a script idea that I had. My professor loved it, thinking it would make an excellent feature film despite its genre, a crime/detective/mystery (this genre tends to work poorly for feature-length films, but is excellent for made-for-television movies). By the end of the course session, I had developed the premise into a full 118-page screenplay intended for the big screen. After reading and rereading it, we determined that it would work much better for the small screen because of the plot choices. Bottom line, it all depends on the execution and development of the premise. Given the importance of premise in all the other areas of a screenplay, I suggest writing your premise down on a Post-it® note or typing and saving it as your desktop wallpaper so that you won't lose focus.

Treatment for Premise Problems

The methods below will help you to assess the premise of your screenplay and ensure that it contains the necessary creative and commercial aspects. These necessary aspects include:

- A clear hero or heroine (the protagonist)
- A clear character goal
- A clear character motivation—a need or reason for attaining the goal
- Originality in execution and development while still capitalizing on recognizable, time-honored, and proven-successful similar ideas

Initially, it will be the *familiarity* of the idea that draws the attention of a buyer, because he or she knows it's a premise that has worked before. But the *originality* of the idea's execution and development will seal the deal. Also remember that the average adult human being's attention span is fifteen to twenty minutes. But agents, producers, and studio executives appear to be nonhuman (given their tumultuous workloads). Therefore, you need to make sure that your premise is deliverable in the shortest way possible.

Along with the protagonist, goal, motivation, and originality, the premise aids in the development of the rest of the story, in particular, obstacles, conflict, and theme.

To aid with identifying, clarifying, and refining your script's premise, you may work it through three successful methods: Posing a "What if?" question, writing a logline, and comparing concepts. Let's look at "What if?" first.

- Posing a "What if?" question for your concept allows you to assess the premise that you already have by its intrigue instead of by its clarity. The "What if?" question also allows you to evaluate the conflict potential—whether or not you and your audience are easily able to see the conflict that may arise out of your character and his or her actions. For instance, if you had been the rewriter for *Billy Madison*, you might have posed the question: What if a grownup went back to grades one through twelve? By just posing this question, you could easily answer: well, this scenario could happen and this scenario could happen . . . and this. . . . Or, what if a groovy spy was cryogenically frozen in the sixties and finally thawed in the nineties to fight evil (*Austin Powers*)?

Ask "What if?" of your screenplay's premise. Then answer the question to see whether there is enough conflict within your story to raise it to its full potential.

- Loglines are a very productive way to focus on your script's premise. A logline is a short (about twenty-five words), simple description of who does what in your story. It presents your character and your character's action. To illustrate, the premise of *The Replacements* is: A bunch of has-been football players serve as replacement players during a professional football strike. Try to write your story premise in as few words as possible so that what you have at the end of those words is a premise that is focused and, above all, catchy. I also think it's important to add a "why" into the logline. So the logline of your story would answer: Who does what in this story and why? It's important to add the "why" so that you and the person potentially buying the script are aware of the character's motivation . . . creating a reason why anyone would care what the character does and, therefore, answering why the script should be read.

    Loglines are also used in addition to treatments and entire screenplays as one of the selling techniques when pitching a script—they must be salable as well as workable.

Write loglines in the present tense, just like treatments and synopses.

- One of the most helpful methods in developing premises and the one I most often use is the movie-cross. Victoria Wisdom, a literary agent for Becsey, Wisdom, and Kalajian, refers to this as "just like, but different." The movie-cross technique takes your script's premise and matches it appropriately with two already-produced scripts. It is a useful method to create a visual picture of the script for yourself or for the person you are pitching it to. I describe one of my scripts as *Silence of the Lambs* meets *Divine Secrets of the Ya-Ya Sisterhood*.

When using the "just like, but different" method, try to focus on the latter part of it (the "but different"). Your script should always have a fresh and unique angle. Since most movies nowadays have borrowed premises, your plot development will distinguish it from the others. Also, use caution when fusing together the two movie premises to describe yours. Ask yourself, does it make sense or does it create an identity crisis for its intended audience as far as genre is concerned?

We've covered premise—let's tackle theme.

Symptoms of a Problem Theme

- Lacks irony
- Overly biased
- Incomprehensible
- Too simplistic
- Too complicated

Simply put, theme is the moral of your story. The premise causes the theme. The theme develops from the premise. The theme grows out of the premise and inadvertently becomes what it is at the end of the story because of the events that unfold throughout the story. Let this natural process happen. Don't inflict the theme upon the premise; instead, let the premise impose the theme upon the story.

The theme is essentially the viewpoint or bias you bring to your story and the internal and external motivations of your characters. It is ironic that both premise and theme derive from logic and reasoning, because emotion is also essential for their effectiveness.

The premise opens the story. You and the audience will know the premise early in the beginning. In contrast, the theme will be naturally discovered at the point of resolution—it unveils itself to the audience as the story progresses.

The theme is the underlying message you ultimately want your script to convey to your audience. The theme of *The Replacements* is that you must seize the opportunity for second chances. The theme can be one of the most difficult parts of your script to define and refine. You may not even know what your theme is yet—which is fine. Perhaps through the course of the rewrite you will be able to determine what it is. Some people believe that not all scripts need a theme because of their genre. In my experience, however, the best scripts *always* have a theme.

Because your script will eventually act as its own marketing tool, you should keep in mind that, when marketing a product, the best campaigns encompass a premise and an angle that thematically brings the package all together. Without the thematic angle, your audience will be apathetic toward what you are trying to sell.

The theme is the coded message that you consciously plant and the audience subconsciously decodes. The theme should resonate through all of the characters and subplots and be interwoven into the premise and plot. The theme should be present in some form in each scene.

A story's theme is subjective—it can very easily mean different things to different people. The various experiences that each individual audience member has had in his or her life influences the way each will interpret your script's theme.

Why does your script need a theme? Because you've created this killer premise, and unless there is some emotional logic for the audience to connect to that premise, the audience will leave the theater apathetic to what they have just seen. So what if a guy builds a house with his son? The theme of *Life as a House* is that what seems broken can be built again with a little effort—whether a relationship with an estranged son, a past romance, a shanty of a house, or amends for an unfortunate accident that robbed an innocent girl of her mobility. But who cares if what seemed broken can be rebuilt again? What does that have to do with the script and audience? Everything! The theme creates a logical and emotional connection to the audience—someone (and I have a feeling a lot more than just someone) in that theater has a relationship on the rocks, unfinished projects, overwhelming debt, a loved one that is ill, or something else that he or she has lost. With a theme, the audience can relate to and engage with the story.

Whatever your theme may be, you want to be careful that you don't let it control your script. Up until now and in the coming chapters, I stress that you must be focused. Now I'm telling you that theme is one aspect you do not want to overfocus on, because it tends to steer your script in the direction of preachy instead of cinematically entertaining.

When I think of preachy scripts, I tend to think that television provides better obvious examples. Think of *The Cosby Show* in the last few years before it went off the air, what I refer to as the "blue couch" years. Instead of being entertaining and funny (which it was for so many years), the show focused on lessons you would learn in school, like history, music, and society. Coming home from a long day at school myself, I just wanted to be entertained; instead, it felt like I had never left school. Even to this day, when I turn on *The Cosby Show* and see the blue couch on the set, I change the channel. The moral or *theme* of this story: Don't let it happen to your script!

Treatment for Theme Problems

In addition to understanding your script's premise, understand the theme. A writer's inability to understand the concept of theme and how to present it is the major cause of theme problems in a script. Therefore, watch a movie in the list below that best matches your script's genre. You may choose to view a movie not on the list below. That is fine, but I encourage you to pick a film you are unfamiliar with, because it will give you a clear, unbiased perspective, unlike what you may have developed through study. Watch the movie and then see if you can decipher the coded message, paying special attention to the resolution, where the theme will be most evident. Next, determine how the movie presents and re-presents the theme. After this exercise, you should be able to do this with your own script. Ask yourself these questions of the films below:

1. Within the climax and resolution, what theme is conveyed?
2. What causes the presentation of this theme?

ACTION: *Lethal Weapon, Speed*
ADVENTURE: *Indiana Jones and the Temple of Doom, Hook*
COMEDY: *The Full Monty, My Big Fat Greek Wedding*
DRAMA: *Rudy, House of Sand and Fog*
EPIC: *Gandhi, Titanic*
FANTASY: *Edward Scissorhands, The Lord of the Rings* (view all the films in the trilogy because they all have different themes)
HORROR: *Scream, I Know What You Did Last Summer*
MUSICAL: *Footloose, Moulin Rouge*
SCIENCE FICTION: *E.T. the Extra Terrestrial, Alien*
THRILLER: *Fatal Attraction, Silence of the Lambs*
WAR: *Born on the Fourth of July, Saving Private Ryan*
WESTERN: *Tombstone, Unforgiven*

CHAPTER 5

Operation Character

> *"The personages in a tale shall be alive, except in the case of corpses, and . . . always the reader shall be able to tell the corpses from the other."*
>
> —Mark Twain

Symptoms of Character Problems

- Stunted growth
- Apathetic and lethargic toward goal
- Not original
- Unconvincing
- Disliked by the audience

SOMETIMES IN MY SCREENPLAY COVERAGES, I will comment on plot first, especially if the script is heavily based on it. In general, however, I usually like to comment on character first, because it seems more sensible to me to know the characters completely before you plot their journeys. After all, the journey is shaped by the character who travels it. Characters are the center of attention. Characters are involved in everything, especially in the point of view and in the action of the story. Characters perform the action, and the action reveals the characters—it's that cause-and-effect relationship again. As Irwin R. Blacker states in his book, *The Elements of Screenwriting*, "A character is developed in relation to other characters; he must act upon, react to, and, in turn, be acted upon by others. He is revealed by encounter, decision, action, and reaction." If the character's actions determine the plot, and characterization determines the actions of the character, then characterization is determined or caused by the goal. That's why it's so important to know each character's goal, especially that of the protagonist.

Like any fiction, characters of a screenplay must be three-dimensional or dynamic, not static, so that the audience will become fully invested in the story and genuinely care about what happens to the characters. Like your characters, the audience members must not be static. That is, of course, the purpose of a film—to have your audience leave emotionally charged in some way. Characters must be proactive to create an audience that is reactive. Dynamic characters resonate through what they do (action), what they say (dialogue), and even what they don't say (subtext). As is true for all parts of a screenplay, the suggestions in this book for refining characters are guidelines, not strict rules. Not every story genre requires in-depth, complicated characters, since the focus may be on other aspects of the story. For instance, action movies do not require overly detailed characters because the focus is on the action. If you are unsure of your script's genre, I suggest you review chapter 7 before reading this chapter. Once you know your script's genre, you will be able to evaluate and refine your characters accordingly.

Are you unsure who counts as a character worthy of the time and effort of evaluation? Here's a trick that script doctors use: thumb through your script and find the characters for whom you took time to describe age, appearance, and so on, and whose names appear frequently. When you spot these characters, you will know that these are the characters who will probably matter in your script, the ones you should spend time on.

Protagonist

A screenplay contains a protagonist who is often dubbed the hero/heroine. In contemporary screenwriting, a protagonist may even be an anti-hero whose flaws and contradictions outweigh his or her strength and power. Nonetheless, the protagonist in a story is a major (or "lead") character. Protagonists are sometimes named in the title (*Billy Madison*), making identifying the protagonist relatively easy. The protagonist aspires to reach a goal that sends him or her and the audience on a journey to achieve that goal. The goal may be physical, emotional, spiritual—it does not matter, as long as the protagonist has a passionate yearning for it in the beginning that gets stronger throughout the course of the script. The protagonist's goal molds the plot.

A well-developed, three-dimensional protagonist will and should connect the audience to the story emotionally. The protagonist should be someone the audience can root for and genuinely care about throughout the journey. But not all protagonists are easily liked. There are good-natured people in our lives we cannot stand and there are ghastly people that somewhere in their vile existence seem to have at least one good quality that we cling to in hopes of their redemption. These character contradictions are what make the characters (especially the protagonist) human, interesting, and easy for the audience to relate to.

There are scripts in which more than one character is striving after the same goal—with an equal amount of desire to reach that goal. If your script is one of these, it may be difficult to determine the protagonist. Here's a hint: the character who makes the decisions or assumes the leadership role, the one the other characters listen to and follow, is the protagonist.

Remember, it is easier for the audience to identify with the protagonist if he or she is introduced early in the script.

Antagonist

The antagonist is the force that directly opposes your protagonist—he or she is the bad guy, villain, monster. Not all antagonists are pure evil, however. In fact, some of the best antagonists possess sympathetic and attractive qualities. But when the antagonist comes close to being more attractive and sympathetic than the hero, it gets dangerous for the effectiveness of the story you are trying to tell.

The antagonist opposes the character physically and/or mentally. Like the protagonist, who has a goal, a good antagonist will have a motive. In addition, the antagonist is also a major or lead character. The antagonist need not be a physical, human entity. If the antagonist is material—human, force of nature, monster— the opposition for the protagonist is called an external opposition. If the antagonist is an inner struggle within the protagonist, the opposition or conflict is called an internal opposition. The tornado in *Twister* serves as the external opposing force for Helen Hunt's character, whereas in the movie *Castaway*, the antagonist could be the island or Chuck himself, as he fights the person inside of him.

Sometimes it isn't just a matter of internal or external antagonist. Some of the best films contain a balance of both. The best combination is the character with an internal conflict as well as a human antagonist, because the human antagonist forces the inner struggle to show itself and can bring out character contradictions that make the characters interesting and believable. Because of the antagonist's oppositional force, the critical conflict arises that drives plot, which we will discuss in the next chapter. Even if the conflict results from a protagonist's internal antagonist, some kind of outside opposition is always present. Vice versa, even with opposition that results from an external antagonist, the protagonist will always have some sort of internal conflict. In *The Karate Kid*, Daniel is the protagonist and his antagonist or opposition is Johnny. Daniel, however, also has an internal conflict to defeat, the anxiety over having balance in all of his relationships and life.

During the discussion on the protagonist, I mentioned that, although the protagonist is the hero or heroine of a screenplay, this does not mean that he or she must be 100 percent likable. Likewise, antagonists need not be 100 percent evil or even evil at all. In fact, the most interesting antagonists (not to mention the most endearing) are the ones that possess deep character contradictions and motives for committing acts of malice. I never really enjoyed movies such as *Friday the 13th* because there seemed to be no logical motive for killing, thus creating a barrier that left me on the outside of the film's reality. To me, devilishly evil antagonists are like politicians. The more passionate, organized, and pleasured by the dirty tricks they commit against their opponents, the more interested I am in them. It doesn't mean that I condone their actions, but I do find them interesting to watch.

In addition to the deep character contradictions and motives that make great antagonists, I find male antagonists who are charismatic and seductive femme fatales who use their powers of persuasion more interesting and effective than blatant evilness. These characters manipulate and seduce in a way that masks their underlying evil from those who fall under their spell. When I think of characters from already produced films that fit this mold, I think of Terry Benedict in *Ocean's Eleven* and Hannibal Lecter in *Silence of the Lambs*. I think others agree with the latter, since the American Film Institute voted Hannibal Lecter the number one film villain of all time.

In *The Italian Job*, Stella (played by Charlize Theron) says, "I trust everyone. It's the devil inside them I don't trust." Some of the best antagonists conceal their wickedness, acting and appearing like normal people. Perhaps this is why serial killers are so intriguing and chilling—they lurk around society unnoticed, and we never know when or where they'll strike next. Think of Harrison Ford in *What Lies Beneath*—I was fooled until the end!

Supporting Characters

There are characters in screenplays who have no specific characteristics or characterizations; they are almost insignificant to the progression of the story or serve a small purpose and then are meant to be forgotten by the audience. Then there are the supporting characters. Supporting characters make up the subplots that weave into the main story plot. Supporting characters serve many purposes. Some of the most popular are comic relief and therapy (a way for the central character to disclose inner thoughts, feelings, and back-story). Like a real-life relationship, the relationship between the central character and the supporting characters may have been formed and sustained through a similar goal, a rivalry, a mutual relationship with a third party, or, in many instances, *opposites attract*. When choosing your supporting characters, choose a garden variety—give each of the characters his or her own characteristics and characterization. This approach will guarantee believability and conflict. Each supporting character must play a significant or a minor role in moving the story forward to its climactic end.

With an ensemble cast and various subplots weaving in and out of the main story, you will notice that each well-developed subplot will have its own so-called protagonist who makes the decisions and whom the other characters follow. In *The Lord of the Rings*, the main story follows Frodo (the protagonist) and his confidant, Sam. One of the subplots follows Aragorn (subplot protagonist) and his confidants Legolas and Gimli (who mostly provides comic relief). Likewise, in the *Star Wars* trilogy, the main story plot follows Luke Skywalker (the protagonist) in pursuit of his goal with his confidant R2-D2; within one of the subplots, C-3PO, Princess Leia, and Chewbacca follow the subplot protagonist, Han Solo.

Wilson in *Castaway* is a supporting character and a contradiction—he is not human but an inanimate object. However, Wilson still changes, as do all supporting characters. Wilson is transformed from an ordinary volleyball into Chuck's companion in a desperate time—he develops (even as an inanimate object) characteristics and characterizations. Moreover, the audience develops feelings/emotions/attachment to Wilson. Wilson is, in a sense, the physical entity of Chuck's alter ego— but someone we the audience, as well as Chuck, have grown very attached to through very skillful writing and the knowledge of what makes a character three-dimensional . . . human or nonhuman. This leads us to the next part of this chapter: character characteristics.

Character Characteristics

You really need to know everything about your characters before you can plot their journey because, as I mentioned before, your characters "cause" the plot of your story. In fact, you must almost know more about your characters than you do about your own family members, best friend, and even yourself. It's good practice to know much more about your characters and their back-stories than will be used in the script and eventually in the film. A good example of someone who knew his characters inside and out is J. R. R. Tolkien. Many books detail the complete histories, biographies, and characterizations that he developed for his numerous characters, but not all of these were revealed in the books and films they appeared in. Bottom line: know your characters inside and out. Whether the information is used or not, it will still greatly enhance the three-dimensionality of your characters.

Dynamic or three-dimensional characters are more than just characteristics such as habits, physical features, language, and idiosyncratic mannerisms. The difference between characteristics and characterization parallels a concept that appears quite often in scripts and is discussed quite frequently in this book—external vs. internal.

Characteristics of a character focus on external traits such as language, style of clothing, habits, facial and body features. Characteristics are your character's physical distinctions. For instance, in *Finding Nemo*, Nemo's underdeveloped fin is one of his external characteristics. Characteristics create real and believable characters because external traits are often related to the internal characterization a character possesses. Dave in *The Full Monty* is a good example of this point. Dave considers himself bald and fat. This fuels his poor self-image, which ultimately affects his intimacy with his wife. This poor self-image motivates him to strip with the other guys in an attempt to prove his desirability.

Character Characterization

Although characteristics are important, you must also provide characterization for your characters. Characterization focuses on the internal matters that define a character. Characterization refers to the depth, dimension, and dynamics of your characters, including the protagonist, the antagonist, and the supporting characters. In addition, characters will require different levels of depth based on the story and genre you have chosen. Nemo's external characteristic (the underdeveloped fin) is what gives These reasons underline why more of your rewrite time will be devoted to characterization. Nemo the inner determination to conquer obstacles that others think he can't. It's not just the presence of the underdeveloped fin that makes Nemo three-dimensional; the underlying motivation of that fin makes him three-dimensional, his mannerisms real, and his actions within the story logical.

As a writer and a rewriter, you must invest time and energy in your characters—such effort will pay off. One of your goals as the rewriter is to evaluate and refine any stereotypical characters who are flat and who will not resonate with your audience. The most important areas to review to determine if your characters are well characterized include:

Goal and motivation. A character becomes three-dimensional when he or she has a clear goal and motivation that are revealed through the conflict and obstacles the character encounters. Emotions such as love, hate, and greed fuel motivation. Motivation should generate all of a character's actions toward his or her goal throughout the story. Often the juxtaposition of two or more emotions create the most intense story and dramatic irony throughout the script. Many things may motivate your characters, including revenge, second chances, and survival.

What the protagonist does to achieve his or her goal when the antagonist is after the same goal heightens the conflict and drama of a script. This is especially true when the antagonist's actions intertwine with those of the protagonist, creating obstacles for the protagonist. Chapter 6 includes more information about obstacles. Your character must have a goal that he or she is trying to reach. This goal may be anything, but it should never be easy to achieve. Why? Because, without opposition toward the goal, there would be no conflict. Without conflict, no characterization would be revealed, and without characterization, your audience will feel no emotional attachment toward the character. And if the audience feels no emotional attachment to your character, they will not be emotionally attached to the plot. If they don't feel a connection to the plot, their rear ends will not be attached to the theater seats. You can now see how one thing influences the other, a domino effect. Character apathy equals audience apathy.

Coinciding with the goal is your character's motivation for attaining that goal. You must understand completely why your character wants what he or she wants. For the character to continue to endure obstacle after obstacle in his or her journey would not be logical without strong motivation.

Back-story. You, the rewriter, should know the entire back-stories of your characters whether the audience knows them or not. The writer determines where and how much back-story will be revealed within the plot, and whether it will be revealed all at once, little by little, in the first scene, or in a flashback.

History and geography. When you refine your characters, be conscious of the era in which you have placed them and of their physical environment. If it takes a course in history or geography to educate yourself and better orient your characters, it is well worth the investment. Just as we are influenced by our place of origin and time in history, so are our characters.

Character Believability

Characters reflect humanity and should, therefore, have human qualities, including emotions, values, flaws, and contradictions. As I mentioned previously, protagonists aren't 100 percent angels. Likewise, antagonists often are not 100 percent devils (depending on the genre, of course). Don't be afraid to give your characters flaws and contradictions—they will only make your characters that much more real and relatable for the audience. For renowned actor Robert Duvall, character contradictions are the first aspects he looks for in a script. With character contradictions, you might want to juxtapose the internal (emotional) conflicts and the external (physical) conflicts in the script. Some films, especially those in the action genre, like *The Terminator*, don't need three-dimensional characters. However, just because a film is of a particular genre doesn't mean that the characters won't be (or shouldn't be, for that matter) well characterized. For example, although episodes IV, V, and VI of *Star Wars* may focus on Darth Vader's pure evilness, you can look at the prequel episodes (I, II, and III) and see a much different array of characters. In these episodes, we can see the character contradictions of Anakin (a.k.a. Darth Vader) and the back-story characterization that contributes to his struggle to choose good over evil, "the dark side." Anakin (in episodes I, II, and III) is a much more three-dimensional character than his alter ego Darth Vader in episodes IV, V, and VI. He has an edge but is not completely evil like Darth Vader. As a result, this shifts the dynamics of the style of story.

Even though several of your characters may possess similar qualities, each character should view and react to situations differently. The difference in their reactions should be based on their back-stories.

What's in a Name?

When parents choose names for their children, they put a lot of time (often the entire nine months of pregnancy) and effort into it to ensure that they pick a name that they not only like, but that is meaningful as well. This lengthy naming process often affects a child throughout the rest of his or her life. Not by the child's choice, his or her name may be associated with positive personality traits such as honor, respect, strength, and purity or with not-so-positive personality traits such as hatred and brutality. I take naming characters very seriously and therefore put a lot of time and effort into it. To me, a name is an investment in a character's personality and, like the attachment to a real child, gives me a sense of ownership and pride. Many people name their children after memorable characters in films, characters with well-developed characteristics, characterization, and symbolism. It is an honor for screenwriters when their characters have such impact on the lives of their audiences.

Again, as a writer, you should put the same time and effort into naming your characters as parents put into the naming of their children. Expending great effort in naming characters should be limited to the protagonist, the antagonist, and the supporting characters. Since the others have very little significance in the story, their names are not as important. As a rewriter, take a look at your characters' names—what do the names reveal or not reveal about them? The first step in assessing what revelation the names of your characters provide is to understand the meaning of certain names so you can determine whether your characters' names accurately represent them. And, if a name doesn't accurately represent a particular character, you can find a name with a meaning that does. To do so, go to your local bookstore and browse the sections on parenting. There you will find an abundance of baby-name books that will list names, their origins, meaning, spelling variations, and sometimes, famous people with a particular name. The only downside to buying baby-name books, especially if you are very young, is that they don't come with bold red lettering on the front cover saying: MAY BE USED FOR PURPOSES OTHER THAN NAMING A BABY. When I started to get serious about writing in high school, I bought a baby-name book and never told my mother. Without thinking, I left it on my bedroom floor. You can pretty much guess her reaction when she saw it lying there!

Character names can also directly reflect nouns—people, places, and things. It's an effective, efficient method of exposition. For instance, Charity, Madison (perhaps if your setting is in Wisconsin or New York City), or Jesus (perhaps your character is a godlike figure).

Character names may also sound like what the character represents, such as Kirk (sounding like and meaning "church") or even Anakin, which sounds like "mannequin" and even subtly implies a machinelike, nonhuman demeanor . . . hmm.

Look to your new, refined story theme for help in finding a name that best represents your characters and story.

Character names can subtly add symbolism and depth to not only the characters, but to the entire story—they bring a sense of unity to the story and may even create dramatic irony. For instance, the character name "Maverick" played by Tom Cruise in *Top Gun* refers to an "independent person in thought and action" and "a resistance toward adhering to a group." The name Maverick suits the character's characterization because Maverick the character bucks the structured system at the naval aviation training school and seems to rebel against his fellow students and superiors. Is this harmony between character name and character characterization a coincidence? I don't think so. Very skilled screenwriters did their research to create a three-dimensional character whose name reinforces his characterization, thus enriching and unifying the entire story. It doesn't matter if the screenwriters fully intended the specific symbolism I see in the name; they could have had other reasons for choosing it. What is important is that good screenplays and films are open to interpretation, possessing enough subtle depth to the characters that audiences experience a deeply emotional cinematic experience.

Character Analysis: *The Lord of the Rings*

No one has developed three-dimensional characters better than J. R. R. Tolkien. Tolkien's immense knowledge of what makes the protagonist, antagonist, and supporting characters fascinating are evident in *The Lord of the Rings*. Moreover, Peter Jackson, Philippa Boyens, and Fran Walsh did a superb job at presenting the depth of Tolkien's characters in his film versions of the trilogy.

Because I have studied the works of Tolkien, particularly *The Lord of the Rings* trilogy, I know that Tolkien knew a great deal more about his characters than could have ever been presented on screen. His knowledge of his characters (inside and out) went beyond even what he wrote in the books. Because of the immensely detailed backgrounds Tolkien imagined, what emerged from his knowledge were characters whose motives and actions are plausible, ensuring character believability and consistent behavior.

Each of Tolkien's characters in *The Lord of the Rings* is like a spice—each adds a little touch of flavoring to the written story and fortunately, in recent years, to the films. The characters in *The Lord of the Rings* are all different from one another. Their differences make their relationships and their interaction dynamic.

Let's take a look at some of the characters in Tolkien's story and Jackson's script. Pay special attention to the depth and detail of each one, keeping in mind how each contributes to the whole. A brief background for each character (a character breakdown) appears below, offering a glimpse into the truth of each character. As you read each mini-biography, look for the things that make a good, well-developed character, such as motivation, name and meaning, background, back-story, and so on.

THE PROTAGONIST

- *Frodo Baggins.* As the protagonist of *The Lord of the Rings*, Frodo holds the fate of Middle-earth in his hands with the task of destroying the One Ring in the fires of Mount Doom. Frodo's name in Old English is Frod and it means "wise." Like Tolkien himself, Frodo was an orphan, adopted by Bilbo Baggins (whom he calls uncle), a cousin sixty years' Frodo's senior. Frodo's internal conflict is great—he longs for stability, yet yearns for excitement and celebrity status, as shown in the interest he takes in Bilbo's adventures. The effect of the climactic end (the destruction of the ring) is Frodo's departure on a ship into the West, to the Undying Lands—leaving behind all that he worked to save.

THE SUPPORTING CHARACTERS

- *Aragorn*. Aragorn, whose name means "Lord of the Trees," is the son of Arathorn and the last descendent of the ancient kings. A commander of sorts, Aragorn leads the forces to destroy the threat of Mordor. Aragorn faces a constant struggle to prove himself worthy of regaining the throne his father left behind. But Aragorn's back-story runs deep. After the Orcs killed her husband, Aragorn's mother brought Aragorn to Rivendell for refuge and so Elrond, Master of Rivendell, could raise him. There he was given yet another name, Estel (Elvish for "hope"), and his true royal identity is concealed from him until Elrond reveals it on his twentieth birthday.

   Aragorn then gets his true name back plus some royal heirlooms, the Ring of Barahir (the ring of friendship) and the shards of Narsil, the sword that Isildur used to slice the hand of Sauron, releasing the One Ring. Aragorn must then earn the throne and prove his worthiness by defeating Sauron and all of Sauron's evil forces. Leaving behind his forbidden love, Arwen (daughter of Elrond), Aragorn sets out on his quest to capture the throne as a Ranger (named Strider), and this is when he enters the first installment of the trilogy, *The Fellowship of the Ring*. Aragorn leads the fellowship in an attempt to get from Rivendell to Mount Doom. When the Hobbits (Merry and Pippin) are captured by Orcs and the fellowship crumbles, Aragorn leads Legolas and Gimli on a quest to rescue the two Hobbits. During the rescue attempt and the battles that follow, Aragorn proves himself a worthy but, more importantly, a noble king.
- *Gandalf*. Gandalf, who is called the "Grey Pilgrim" or "Gandalf the Grey" by the Elves, is loyal to his allegiances. Gandalf is a mentor of sorts to Frodo and Aragorn, especially. Along with his admirable traits, including wisdom, compassion, and self-control, Gandalf has a short temper

(shown when he is around the troublemaker Hobbit, Pippin). Mirroring Christ, Gandalf sacrifices his life for Middle-earth and the fellowship when he faces the Balrog. In addition, The Valor from the Undying Lands of the West send him back to Middle-earth even more powerful than he left it, so he becomes known as "Gandalf the White." This resurrection also mirrors the resurrection of Christ. Only after his mission to destroy Sauron and restore the King of Gondor (Aragorn) does Gandalf return to the West with Elrond, Galadriel, Bilbo, and Frodo.

Gandalf's back-story includes servanthood, including with the Vala Lórien and Vala Nienna (the Lady of the Mourning), during which he learned most of his admirable qualities. His most powerful affiliation is his servanthood to the Secret Fire or the "Flame of Anar" (the sun), which he uses to illuminate, compared to the "Flame of Udûn," used to cast shadows. There is a direct correlation between good and evil and light and dark with Gandalf.

- *Samwise "Sam" Gamgee.* Keeping his promise to Gandalf, Sam pledges his loyalty to his employer and friend Frodo on the journey to destroy the One Ring in Mount Doom. There is a clear relationship arc between Frodo and Sam. In the beginning, their relationship is businesslike—employer/employee, served/servant. By the end, the distinction between classes is replaced by a strong, neverending friendship. In Old English, Samwise means "half-wise," and his greatest trait is keeping his promise. Sam is a bit of a dreamer—wanting to meet the Elves, to go on wild adventures much like Bilbo, and perhaps to secure a mention or two of his name in great tales in the years to come.

Although Sam possesses more heroic qualities, Frodo remains the protagonist in *The Lord of the Rings* because he makes the decisions and the others follow his lead—Frodo holds the power, both literally and metaphorically.

- *Legolas.* Legolas, whose name means "Green Leaf," is the son of King Thranduil and is Prince of the Woodland

Elves. Loyal to Aragorn and Gimli in their quests, with his keen eyesight and hearing and his flawless skill with the bow, Legolas proves his worth in critical situations. While his friendship with Aragorn is apparent and consistent, the relationship arc between Legolas and Gimli develops in an interesting manner—they move from distrusting, intolerant acquaintances to loyal, tolerant friends, demonstrating the underlying theme of their relationship, that differences can be overcome.

- *Gimli.* Gimli's size is no indication of his bravery and his role in saving Middle-earth. Gimli provides (as do Merry and Pippin) comic relief, especially in such instances as the Orc-killing competition between him and Legolas and his discussion with Éowyn about Dwarf distinctions during the migration to Helm's Deep in *The Two Towers.*

  Because of the Elves' longtime mistrust of the Dwarves, Gimli and Legolas don't get along at first. However, by the end, they become friends and Gimli proves his trustworthiness through his loyalty in battle.

- *Merry and Pippin.* Because of time constraints, Merry and Pippin were not as developed in the movies as they were in the books. Nonetheless, they still play valuable roles in saving Middle-earth. Just because their screen time doesn't depict their complete dimensionality does not mean it doesn't exist. Pippin is Frodo's second cousin, once removed. Moreover, he is hyper (ADHD perhaps?) and outspoken, often getting himself into troublesome situations. Feeling a sense of obligation and revealing his loyalty, Pippin pledges himself to Denethor, the Steward of Gondor, after Denethor's son Boromir is killed.

  Merry, a very good friend of Frodo, is self-conscious (particularly about his size) and unsure of the benefit of his presence in the quest to destroy the One Ring. Merry does indeed prove his worth (and that size doesn't matter) in the battle at Pelennor Fields.

  Like Gimli, Merry and Pippin serve as comic relief while still playing serious roles within the story. Their humor is often revealed through their curiosity (character-istic of Hobbits) and other antics. However, the two Hobbits display nobility and loyalty on a journey that takes them on a character arc from fearful, typically apprehensive Hobbits to courageous, life-saving forces. The juxtaposition of Merry and Pippin's individual characterizations (Pippin's cunning and Merry's planning and organization) truly enriches the story.

- *Elrond.* Half-elven, Elrond is the son of Eärendil, a mortal, and Elwing. A twin to brother Elros, Elrond himself has three children with Galadriel's daughter: Elladan, Elrohir, and Arwen. Elrond is the Master of Rivendell, and he fre-quently offers hospitality to those traveling, in danger, or ill.
- *Arwen.* The daughter of Elrond, Arwen's name means "Daughter of Twilight." Arwen faces the constant struggle between the rite of passage (Elvish immortality) and the fate of mortality should she continue to love Aragorn.
- *Éowyn.* Éowyn is a feminist of Middle-earth and of her time. She is skilled with a blade and displays that skill in the fight to save Minas Tirith, even though she is forbidden to go to battle. Éowyn is the niece of King Théoden of Rohan and the sister to Éomer, and her name means "Horse Friend." Although their relationship is not developed much in the films, Éowyn falls in love with and marries Faramir.

ANTAGONIST AND VILLAINS

Who really is the antagonist in *The Lord of the Rings*? Is it Sauron? Saruman? The Orcs? The One Ring? Gollum? All of these seem logical antagonists because they each do what an antagonist should—create opposition for the protagonist during his or her pursuit of reaching the goal. A book could be written on just the theories of who or what is the true trilogy antagonist. If you ask me, I would say that Sauron and his One Ring are the true antagonists. Saruman, the Orcs, the Ringwraiths, Shelob the spider, Gollum, and the other creatures are merely minions of Sauron and the One Ring. But my opinion on who

Tolkien meant as the antagonist is not the point. The point is that, just like the protagonist and supporting characters of *The Lord of the Rings*, Tolkien's (and, more recently, Jackson's) villains are every bit as developed and effective as the other characters through their superb characterization. Here are *The Lord of the Rings's* villains:

- **Sauron.** Sauron, whose full name is Sauron Gorthaur, is the epitome of a great villain. He was not born evil (much like Anakin Skywalker in *Star Wars*). Sauron actually was a servant or an apprentice to a Valar Master, much like a blacksmith. From the Valar Master, Sauron learned to forge. Unfortunately, Sauron then met Melkor, the "Lord of the Might and Darkness." Melkor is hardly mentioned in *The Lord of the Rings* trilogy, but he dominates *The Silmarillion*. Combining the evil he learned from Melkor and the forging skill he learned from the Valar Master, Sauron instructed the Elves in creating the Rings of Power (three for the Elven Masters, seven for the Dwarves, and nine for the mortal kings of men). In addition, Sauron instructed the Elves to create an additional ring—for himself—the One Ring that controlled all the others.
- **The Ringwraiths.** The Ringwraiths or Black Riders were all men at one time—Lords, to be exact. After Sauron gave them each a ring of power, their fear of death and their obsession with immortality caused them to fall victim to the One Ring. The Ringwraiths are filled with hatred. As Sauron's servants, they will stop at nothing to retrieve the One Ring for their master.
- **Shelob.** Shelob is the mammoth spider Frodo encounters after Gollum tricks him into her lair. Shelob is the offspring of Ungoliant, who is also primarily referenced in *The Silmarillion*, and *The Hobbit*. Shelob acts as a security guard, killing and eating all those who try to pass Cirith Ungol into Mordor. What is unique about Shelob is her distaste for light, which is evident when Frodo uses the light of

Eärendil's star, given to him by Galadriel in *The Fellowship of the Ring.* What makes this a unique characterization is the paralleling irony: Ungoliant craved light—an addiction completely opposite from her daughter's.

- *Orcs.* The Orcs are, in theory, Sauron's soldiers. The Orcs are former Elves, captured and tortured by Melkor. Bred maliciously, the Orcs are disfigured but relentless soldiers. Despite their ruthless ways and frightening demeanors, the Orcs do have one significant weakness—their sensitive skin, which only allows them to fight during the night. To combat this flaw, Saruman breeds a different variation of Orc, the Uruk-hai, who are not sensitive to light and therefore can fight at all hours of the day.

- *Saruman.* Saruman's name means "crafty-man," and that he was through his creation of weapons and an Orc army. When Tolkien first introduced the character Saruman in *The Silmarillion*, his purpose in the story was to help people. But Saruman inevitably succumbed to the power of the One Ring, longing for it in an attempt to control and strengthen his powers. Saruman might be perceived as a land developer—driving out the living creatures and having no respect for nature. Sweet justice comes to Saruman, however, when Treebeard and the Ents destroy his underground cache and hold him prisoner on his own land at Isengard.

- *Gollum/Sméagol.* Oh, how to categorize Gollum? Is he a villain or is he a supporting character? The very quandary is what makes Gollum such a great villain. Gollum is not pure evil; he was born kind-hearted. Gollum is the perfect example of the One Ring's power to twist and distort (both physically and mentally) the very beings that encounter and possess it. Because the audience knows that Gollum is influenced and therefore a victim to the One Ring, they pity him. Audiences sympathize with Gollum and endure his pain while he struggles from good and bad throughout the journey. Gollum, whose real name is Sméagol, was much like a Hobbit. While fishing with Déagol, Déagol snagged the Ring of Power from the depths of the water. Immediately succumbing to the One Ring's power, Sméagol yearns for the ring and wrestles with Déagol to get it. When Déagol refuses to give the ring to Sméagol, Sméagol kills Déagol. After the murder, Sméagol is banished from his home and family. Under the One Ring's spell, Sméagol becomes sensitive to sunlight and withers in the shadows of the mountains. As his body disfigures and decays, he begins choking on his own phlegm and is henceforth called Gollum, for the noise he makes. Quite a back-story, huh?

As you can tell from each character described above, J. R. R. Tolkien put a great amount of time, research, and effort into each of his characters. A researcher and scholar, Tolkien based many of characters on the ancient mythologies he studied—Greek, Roman, and Norse, specifically. You may have noticed that I did not list Bilbo Baggins, Boromir, Faramir, King Théoden, Treebeard, Éomer, and Galadriel, among others. They were not included because I couldn't, within the realm of this book, begin to discuss all of the critical characters in *The Lord of the Rings*—there are too many. However, many wonderful sources focus on the complete analysis of each character. You may have noticed that there is more than meets the eye here, not just in the films, but in the books as well. Tolkien didn't just develop one character, he developed that "one" character's father, mother, siblings, children, extended family, and more. In fact, Tolkien has developed so many characters related to each other and with full backgrounds that he provides genealogy charts for them!

Conclusions we can draw from the *Lord of the Rings* character breakdowns are:

- They all have characteristics and characterizations that shape them into unique individuals, each vital to the story. These characteristics and characterizations include, but are in no way limited to, their names, physical features, relationships, and social status.

- All of the characters have a clear motivation. They are not satisfied with complacency and their actions reflect that.
- All of them have a clear purpose or reason for being involved in the plot. In addition, each has internal and external conflicts taking place throughout the story.
- The supporting characters, in addition to the protagonist (Frodo), have a character arc. They evolve from what they are in the beginning to something different in the end.
- The villains, particularly Gollum, are not pure evil, yet they are in complete conflict with the hero(es), as any good antagonist should be.
- Because they have distinct backgrounds, races, and past experiences, the action of each character stems from his or her own point of view in the story. Aragorn's reasons for defending Middle-earth differ from Merry and Pippin's reasons, for example. Unlike the audience, the characters are oblivious to the role the others play—as far as each is concerned, each believes and acts like he or she is the main character.
- The objectives of the supporting characters do not over-power or derail the protagonist or his or her objective. Despite all that is happening with Aragorn, Gimli, Legolas, Merry, Pippin, Treebeard, Gandalf, Faramir, King Théoden, the Elves, Arwen, Sam, and Gollum, they and we the audience still follow and root for Frodo and his struggle to destroy the One Ring and save Middle-earth from darkness.

Treatment of Character Problems

Based on what you have read about characters above, go through your script and find your major and supporting characters. When you have done so, the next step is to create a character breakdown sheet. In most of my service packages, I offer my clients a breakdown of their characters. Character breakdowns serve many people in the film industry. Sometimes I receive scripts from agencies that are submitted with a certain actor or actress in mind, and they need to know all of the various roles available. One constant remains, however: whether for an agent, production company, casting agency, or independent writer, character breakdowns are valuable to the rewriting process because they allow you to see, even if briefly, the three-dimensionality or lack thereof of a character.

Character breakdowns range in length from about half a page to two pages, depending on the number of characters in the script, who is requesting it, what it will be used for, and whether all characters are covered.

The order of the character breakdown begins with the most substantial roles, or "leads," as they are called in film, followed by the supporting characters and, if you choose to include them, the minor characters in your script.

Within each of these character listings, you should mention the character's name, age, physical attributes, and, if pertinent, the character's back-story.

Here is an example of a character breakdown:

CASSI LAKE, early thirties and tiny build. She has chocolate brown hair with a hint of mahogany and sun-kissed skin. Considering herself a conservative, she is a private investigator by trade; however, her true passion lies with art and painting. Cheated on by her (then) fiancé seven years prior, She remains a skeptical, guarded person, yet a compassionate and attentive mother to her daughter, SAMANTHA.

This description covers the following areas:

Name: Cassi
Age: Early thirties
Physical attributes: Tiny build, chocolate brown hair with a tint of mahogany and sun-kissed skin.

In addition, this description delivers information regarding:

Politics: Conservative
Hobbies/Interests: Art and painting
Personality: Skeptical, guarded, compassionate, and attentive
Back story: Cheated on seven years ago by her fiancé
Responsibilities: Mothering a child

To achieve this type of description, you should know and understand all of the physical, technical, social, private, unconscious, and fun elements that comprise your characters.

Physical

NAME *(first, middle and last)*:

GENDER:

AGE:

HEIGHT: WEIGHT:

HAIR COLOR:

EYE COLOR:

HANDICAP(S):

ETHNICITY:

STYLE OF DRESS:

FITNESS:

Technical

PLACE OF RESIDENCE:

MARITAL STATUS:

FINANCIAL STATUS:

SEXUAL ORIENTATION:

EDUCATION:

OCCUPATION:

Social

POLITICAL LEANINGS:

INTERESTS AND HOBBIES:

FRIENDS: *(names, length of friendship, how the relationship was formed)*:

NICKNAME: USED BY:

LOYALTIES/RESPONSIBILITIES:

RELIGIOUS IDENTIFICATION:

INTIMACY
      WITH LOVERS:
      WITH FRIENDS:
      WITH FAMILY:

SUPERSTITIONS:

PET PEEVES:

Private

SECRETS:

ADDICTIONS:

PHOBIAS:

GOALS AND AMBITIONS
      CAREER:
      RELATIONSHIP:

Unconscious

FEAR(S):

NEED(S):

FLAW(S):

Fun

FAVORITE COLOR:

TRANSPORTATION: *(car, bus, helicopter, plane, etc.)*:
        MAKE:
        YEAR:
        MODEL:
        COLOR:
        TWO OR FOUR DOOR:

PET(S)
        KIND:
        NAME:

FAVORITE SONG:

FAVORITE MOVIE:

FAVORITE FOOD:

FAVORITE SPORT:

If you are still having trouble with your characters after the breakdown and character guide, then your next step in refining your characters is to research, research, research—observe, observe, observe. A common misconception about conducting research is that you should do it before writing the screenplay. Not so. Research is very much an ongoing process. When you begin the arduous task of researching a topic, you already know *something* about the subject. Researching is adding to or backing up the information you already know about the topic. Hence, think of it as re-searching, just like *re*writing or *re*fining. You aren't starting from scratch; have confidence in what you already know and take it step-by-step from there.

When you observe others, you are looking for a character prototype or example. Look at people for ideas that would serve as prototypical characteristics and characterizations for your characters in the areas of physical description, technical expertise, social experience, private life, unconscious motivations, and fun. The observation and research you conduct is, in essence, the same research actors conduct to better understand the characters they are portraying. For instance, Kurt Russell spent a lot of time with late hockey coach Herb Brooks before and during the filming of the movie *Miracle* so that he could capture the essence and persona of the legend he was portraying.

You can conduct your research anywhere . . . anywhere people are, that is. Just remember to bring along recording supplies to jot down all of your observations. Interviews, too, are an excellent way to conduct accurate character research. A couple of years ago I wrote a screenplay in which both the protagonist and antagonist were hockey players. I love hockey and know a lot about it, but I wanted to make sure that I captured the "true" hockey player so that my characters were as compelling as they could be. I interviewed Jon Cullen, cousin of Matt Cullen of the Carolina Hurricanes and the then-captain of my hometown's WCHA hockey team, the St. Cloud State University Huskies. I bought Jon dinner at the local Applebee's and put him through some very grueling and private questions—while recording his answers as he ate his sizzling fajita. By the end of the dinner, I learned some interesting tidbits and felt I knew and understood my character better.

No one knows people better than psychologists and psychiatrists, so you may want to interview these people. They may help to offer some profiles and generalizations about the way people react and interact with one another and why or what causes a person to act a certain way.

Taking your research a step further and deeper, a great way to assess whether your character is extroverted or introverted, creative or analytical, right-brained or left-brained, is to take the Keirsey test and/or the Myers-Briggs test. Take the tests as if you were your character or have someone that serves as your character's prototype take the test.

The Myers-Briggs Type Indicator was created by Katharine Cook-Briggs and her daughter, Isabel Briggs-Myers, during World War II. It was developed to indicate a person's psychological type, and was based on the work of C. G. Jung, a Swiss psychiatrist who wrote *Psychological Types*. Today, the Myers-Briggs

Type Indicator is the most popular means of deciphering and comprehending personality differences. I have never personally taken the Myers-Briggs Type Indicator, but my husband did during his MBA program. Having never taken a personality test, he learned quite a lot of interesting information about himself (most of which I already knew).

Although I have never taken the Myers-Briggs, I took the Keirsey Temperament Sorter during a business writing course required while obtaining my undergraduate degree. My professor at the time administered the test in an attempt to help us learn more about ourselves so we could choose appropriate career paths.

According to the official website, the Keirsey Temperament Sorter was "created to help people gain new understanding of their traits, motivations, and behaviors; it [the temperament sorter] analyzes one particular aspect of personality: temperament." According to the Keirsey Temperament Sorter, there are four temperaments (or dispositions) of a human being: Artisans, Guardians, Idealists, and Rationals. When I took the test, I was found to be an idealist and didn't disagree with any part of the description. You can find more information on the Keirsey and Myers-Briggs tests on their websites: www.keirsey.com and www.myersbriggs.org.

Within the best stories, the most interesting and three-dimensional characters change in some way from the beginning to the end of the story—the character arc. Like theme, the character change is completed at the end of the script when the protagonist makes the final decision of the story that resolves the conflict, where the ultimate character motivation (want or need) wins.

The character evolves through the conflict and obstacles of the script. This, incidentally, is why the character arc parallels and resembles the plot. Ask yourself:

- Does my character change by the end of the script?
- In what ways does my character change?
- Where within the story does my character change?

CHAPTER 6

Operation Structure and Plot

"Plot is more than a pattern of events: it is the ordering of emotions."

—Irwin R. Blacker

Symptoms of Structure and Plot Problems

- Predictable
- Confusing
- Unbelievable
- Boring
- Lacks originality
- Lacks conflict
- Lacks urgency
- Unbalanced pacing
- Poorly transitioned act breaks
- Inconsistent
- Weak subplot(s)

HAVING A WELL-CONSTRUCTED SCRIPT structure only compliments your story and forces the audience into a participatory role. Good structure engages the audience by presenting a focused story, paced in such a way that makes it interesting and intriguing.

Turning points, conflict, subplots, etc., make up the plot. Basically, structure is the organization of plot. However, there should be a balance between structure and spontaneity—each page of your script should contain an element of interest and surprise—within reason.

I created a chart that compares the structure and plotting of a script with the rhythmic image of a heartbeat—similar to what you might find on an electrocardiogram. I compare the structure and plot of a screenplay to a heartbeat because structure and plot keep the script alive and the story flowing, just like the human heart. Without structure, your script will flatline, as will your audience. You will understand why the heartbeat model is the best representation of structure and plot through the individual figures that coincide with the discussion of each act that follows. Notice that the act divisions of the heartbeat model follow the 1:2:1 ratio and that each plot point thrusts the story in a different direction—while still progressing forward.

Plays and television scripts may contain different numbers of acts—one, five, or seven acts. But screenplays use the three-act structure, which is relatively simple to write. The three-act structure tells the story in a way that helps the audience engage with it and react to it; it best reflects and compliments the thought processes of the audience.

Screenplays have a beginning (Act I), a middle (Act II), and an end (Act III). Each act performs a different role in the script. To get from act to act, the screenwriter employs an action-turning event, typically called a "turning point." Turning points help maintain the script's intrigue and unpredictability. Essentially, a turning point creates a rollercoaster effect within the story to engage the audience. The twists, turns, and drops of a turning point provoke anticipation, intensity, and thrill, which is more interesting than a carousel, which maintains an even pace and consistent, one-direction movement.

I have had several clients base their stories on a linear plot model. When they received their feedback from me, my main area of concern was the plot. The definition of linear is "of, relating to, or resembling a straight line." Although a story should always move forward, it should be anything but straight. The dictionary also mentions that "linear" refers to "only having one

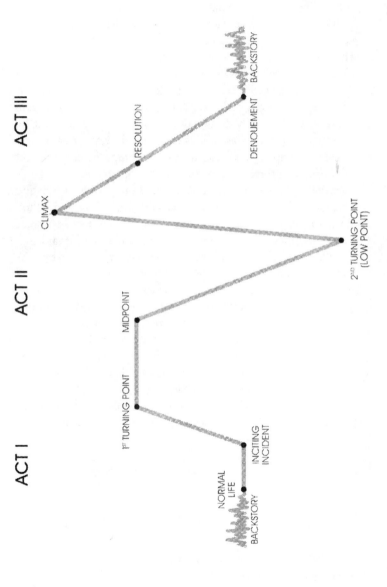

dimension and is characterized by, comprised of, or emphasizing drawn lines rather than painterly effects." There are two critical problems here pertaining to screenplays. The first half of the statement means that a linear structure will certainly affect the characters in a script. Why? Because if the structure is one-dimensional, your characters will be as well. If you think you want to build a script around a linear model, the second part of the statement should talk you out of it. A script should always show instead of tell; it should be visually cinematic, and be approached as an art as well as a science. Linear structure will affect the script by molding it into something mechanical and scientific. The three-act structure is limiting and defining; however, when based on the actions and situations of interesting characters, it actually enhances creativity. The linear method doesn't take your characters on a rollercoaster journey. Instead, it just takes them on a not-very-interesting static trip forward.

The setup of the story occurs in the first act, followed by conflict in the second act, and the resolution of conflict in the third act. Once you set up the story for the audience, you owe them— you must deliver on what you started. In other words, you must resolve any conflicts you set up for your characters.

The ending of each act and the beginning of the next is a subconscious transition for the audience. Although you, the writer, know where the definitive lines are between each act, the lines for the audience are invisible, making the story experience for the audience one of subconscious cohesion. Although a screenplay is composed of separate acts, the separate acts create a unified story.

Character + Goal (Causes) = Plot (Effect)

Within your script, your central character has both a conscious goal and an unconscious goal. I like to say that the central character has a want and a need. The want is what your character physically struggles for, as does the antagonist. Subconsciously, your character has a need that runs parallel to the want, such as (but not limited to) acceptance, love, respect. The need does not usually surface for the character or for the audience until just before the climax, because some sort of character flaw caused by something in the character's back-story suppresses it. For instance, in the movie *Wall Street*, Bud Fox's want is to become a big-shot stockbroker on Wall Street, to have control, power, and money, as does his antagonist, Gordon Gekko. Bud Fox's subconscious need is for love and acceptance from his father. Bud's character flaw is greed, caused by an event that occurred at some point before Stanley Weiser and Oliver Stone started writing the script.

Plot-driven and Character-driven Stories

Either the plot or the character drives a screenplay. In other words, the story develops and focuses either around the plot or around the character. You will want to determine the driving force of your screenplay so that you plot the story accordingly.

If your script is driven by plot, it will focus on your central character's goal and the action that coincides with achieving that goal.

In a plot-driven script, the action is the focus instead of the character. Because the plot-driven story focuses on the plot, the characters ultimately tend to be static. Good examples of plot-driven, static characters are James Bond or, in more contemporary times, any movie starring Vin Diesel.

In contrast, if your screenplay is driven by character, it will focus on the softer side of the story and the plot will revolve around such aspects as relationships. This distinction is similar to and often parallels the two most popular types of premise, high and low concept. Plot-driven stories usually fall into action, science fiction, horror, and other high-concept categories. Character-driven stories tend to be low concept films, such as dramas.

Differing from a plot-driven story, a character-driven story plot focuses on the character(s) before the story's action. The character-driven story is emotionally deeper, thus allowing and inspiring the character(s) to experience a character transformation or character arc. The characters in a character-driven story are significantly different at the end of the story than they were in the beginning. Therefore, character-driven stories focus on the internal conflict of the character(s) and hinge on ambiguity instead of certainty—character-driven stories are painted in shades of gray instead of black and white.

You should stay true to the style of writing with which you are most comfortable. Plot-driven stories are no better and no worse than character-driven stories. Both types appeal differently to different audiences and tend to fit into the realms of certain genres (which we will discuss in chapter 8), genres you may already be accustomed to and enjoy writing in. The characteristics of the two types of stories correspond to the characteristics of the genres with which they are most associated. In addition, different genres tend to appeal to different audiences. To ensure your success in the marketplace, it is important that you know the demographic and industry-specific characteristics of plot-driven and character-driven stories.

Because plot-driven stories appeal to a very wide audience, they tend to be very commercial and successful at the box office—just the way blockbusters should be. But the budget required to produce such films runs from moderate to extremely high. This differs from character-driven stories, where budgets tend to be low, allowing them to appeal to both major studios and to the independent marketplace. Adding to the inflation or deflation of a script's budget are the elements attached to the script. Moreover, essential to the blockbuster, plot-driven stories are more likely to attach elements such as directors and actors/actresses, thus appealing directly to the studio buying the script. However, character-driven stories allow the talents of the actors and actresses to shine. For this reason, character-driven stories directly appeal to many actors and actresses.

Pacing the Acts

Some would argue that writers who follow a strict structure and plot formula greatly risk endangering the originality of their script. Although it's possible for writers to ignore the usual structure of a screenplay and to create a cohesive script, the typical formula should not be overlooked. In addition, a well-structured script prevents predictability, enhances believability, and encourages continuity.

Because of variables like genre and the writer's status in the industry, scripts vary in length. However, unless you have a very good reason to elongate your script, a screenplay should only run about 90–120 pages, or about 90–120 minutes (since one page equals about one minute of screen time). If you followed chapter 3 and deleted scenes that do not belong but still find yourself with a script that is over 120 pages, you need to delete more. Material is deleted not just to make a better script, but for financial reasons as well. The longer the screenplay, the more expensive the film is to make. The more expensive the film is to make, the greater the potential loss—often in the millions of dollars.

A screenplay is no different from any other written document—the tighter and more concise it is, the more effective it is. I have witnessed many formulas that break down the length of a screenplay, but I have found the combination that best fits its three-act structure is roughly the 1:2:1 ratio. So, if your script is 120 pages (or 120 minutes) long, the first act would be about 30 pages/minutes; the second act, 60 pages/minutes; and the third act, another 30 pages/minutes. Remember, these are guidelines and not rules, so your script may vary from this ratio. In fact, scripts for most films used to be 120 pages, but because of decreasing audience attention spans and budget cuts, many scripts now tend to be around 110 pages. Many films targeted toward children (animated or not) run about 90 minutes, since children have shorter attention spans. If you've ever taken a four-year-old to a movie, you know that even 90 minutes can seem like you're watching *Titanic* with them.

Pacing the three acts of a screenplay is like running a cross-country race. When the race gun blasts in act one, you want to start fast and with a bang, hooking your audience instantly. In act two, you will want to settle into a pace, surging when needed through your conflict and plot points in order to progress forward to the finish line—act three. Where you will quicken your pace substantially and push it hard to the end, where you can almost hear your fans' (the audience's) cheers, anxiety, and anticipation for your finish.

In addition, pacing the three-act structure of the script can be accomplished by moving between action scenes and dialogue scenes and between deep-hearted scenes and light-hearted scenes. A pattern develops within well-paced scenes; positive events follow negative events followed by positive events and so on. High points follow low points—always keeping the roller-coaster ride interesting.

ACT I

The first act is the beginning or "takeoff" of the rollercoaster, much like the Aerosmith Rockin' Rollercoaster at Walt Disney World's MGM Studios. The Rockin' Rollercoaster rushes from 0 to 60 mph in 2.8 seconds.

Act one deals with such things as back-story, story question, location, setting, and the introduction of characters. It is the audience-orientation act and sets up the story for the events to come in acts two and three. The first act answers who, what, when, where, and how. Seeds are planted that will need to be watered in the second act so they can fully bloom at the end. In other words, the main character and the character's goal are set forth in act one.

The character and the audience enter the story in the middle of normal, everyday life. But something has happened to the central character at some point in his or her life long before we enter the story—this is the character's back-story. Think of Clarice Starling's back-story in *Silence of the Lambs*.

Likewise, because life is cyclical, new stories begin where great stories end . . . and so the cycle begins again. This is where sequels are born. Think of the line in one of the last scenes in *Meet the Parents*. Dina says: "Well, now it looks like we have another wedding to plan," and Jack responds: "Just gotta do one

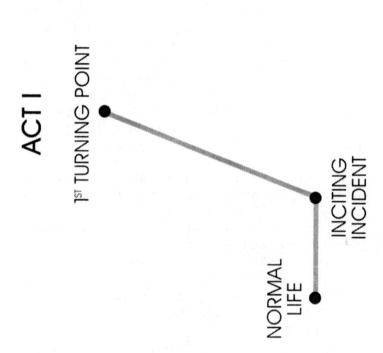

more thing . . . meet his parents." Not only does this line and scene bring us full circle with the premise of *Meet the Parents*, it also sets up the next story to come . . . and *Meet the Fockers* is born. But *Meet the Fockers* doesn't begin immediately after that line; much more has happened in the Focker/Burns families' lives before the first scene of the sequel.

You want to capture the audience's attention within the first ten minutes of the script. If you can, try to capture it within the first scene and use image rather than dialogue. This capture is called the "hook." In a screenplay entitled *The Garnet*, written by a particularly talented client of mine, the client created the hook of her mystery/suspense screenplay within the first scene. It is an obvious murder scene involving two people—blurred images and voices make it impossible to determine the sex of the two people arguing. Audience members hear a loud noise but are unable to determine its cause. Immediately after the noise, they see a blurred image fall to the ground and red liquid (blood) fills the screen. The scene is intriguing and creepy, it sets the mood, and makes me want to know who was murdered, who the murderer is, and why the person was murdered. Mission accomplished. After reading the first scene, I wanted to continue reading. I was hooked. Immediately after the opening scene, the screenwriter introduces Cassi (a private investigator and the protagonist). Remember, you want to introduce your protagonist and any other important characters as soon as possible.

The first thing that happens in the first act is the inciting incident or, as some industry professionals call it, the catalyst. I mentioned before that the character's goal should be established in the first act. Thus, the inciting incident is what introduces the goal for the character. Something happens to him or her that creates a problem, a need, or a desire. The inciting incident jump-starts the story. For Cassi, the *Los Angeles Times* newspaper arrives (also orienting the audience to location and setting), displaying in the headline that the governor has been murdered.

The inciting incident is typically not the same as the first act turning point or plot point. I think of the inciting incident as a bump in the road, whereas the first turning point is an event that skyrockets the story. The inciting incident also creates the hovering story question—the question that will be posed in the beginning and finally answered at the climax and end. Will Billy inherit the family business? Will Cassi solve the murder?

The inciting incident can be an accident, death, explosion, a new neighbor moving in, or a medical diagnosis, just to name a few. For instance, George finds out that he has terminal cancer in *Life as a House*, causing him to want to build a house with his estranged and volatile son. If your screenplay is around 120 pages and the first act is around 30 pages, the inciting incident will usually occur between pages ten and fifteen. In *Life as a House*, George finds out about his cancer around the seventeen minute mark (17 pages).

The first turning point is the point of no return for the character . . . it is where the character commits him- or herself to the journey and the challenge of achieving the goal. The first turning point moves the first act into the second act.

ACT II

Act two tends to give writers and rewriters the most trouble. In act two, your script should deal with rising action plot points, obstacles, conflict, character growth, subplots, and pace. Act two juxtaposes plot and character. The plot intensifies as the protagonist struggles to overcome the obstacles and conflict that stand in the way of his or her pursuit of the goal. Act two is the middle of the story and, as such, should be the longest part of the three-act structure. It is the end of the beginning and the beginning of the end.

When the character commits to his or her goal during the first turning point in act one, the character is thrust into the conflict and obstacles of the second act. Conflict and obstacles are what stand in the way of the protagonist achieving the goal and what the protagonist must overcome. Your character should encounter various kinds of conflict throughout act two, such as conflict

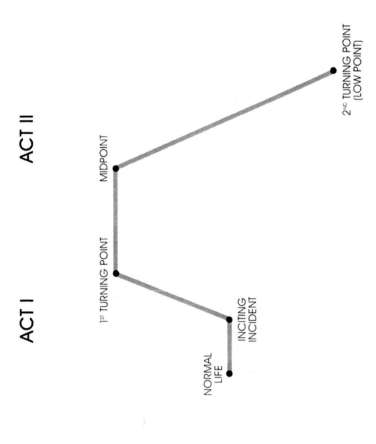

between the protagonist and the antagonist, conflict between the protagonist and nature, conflict between the protagonist and humanity. All of these conflicts are external. A conflict can also be internal, the conflict between the protagonist and him- or herself. In reality, most people hate conflict and avoid it at all cost. However, audiences love experiencing it on screen and must encounter it in your characters and in your story.

A common misconception is that conflict must be violent or huge—not true. In *Tommy Boy*, after a frustrating and unsuccessful day selling brake pads, Tommy wants chicken wings at a local café, but the unenthusiastic waitress refuses to fire up the grill for him (conflict). At this point, it appears that Tommy has lost the battle to get his wings until he inadvertently uses his power sales pitch and persuades the waitress to start the grill (overcoming conflict). This scene not only has its own objective (to get the wings) and conflict, like every well-developed scene should have, but also serves as a necessary scene in the movie. It moves the plot forward by giving Tommy a newfound confidence in his attempt to sell brake pads and save his father's company. Again, goals and objectives are sources of conflict but neither requires complexity or grandeur in the screenplay.

Conflict and obstacles go together. In the second act, the characters must race against a ticking clock, creating suspense and anxiety for them and causing the audience to wonder whether the character(s) will reach the goal. In this act, intensifying, accelerated action and progressive complications make it hard for the character(s) to reach the goal. The obstacles may be anything, physical or emotional. When I ran track in high school and college, if I wasn't mentally preparing for my race, I would try to watch other events or races that were going on. There were some races I didn't care to look at, like the 3200-meter race—eight times around a track. But the races I never missed watching were those involving hurdles. I couldn't do hurdles, but I loved watching others attempt it. Runners leaping the hurdles always kept me on edge—the races were intense. I once had a teammate who was in first place trip over a hurdle, break her ankle, pick herself up, and finish the race. Wow, what inspiration! This is exactly how the audience views the obstacles you place in front of the character in the run for his or her goal. The audience wants and needs to see the character overcome obstacles. There must be a balance of difficulty in the obstacle for the character. Not too easy to overcome, but not impossible, either. Although I felt that hurdles were impossible for me to do, they are in fact height positioned and staggered in a way that makes them possible—much like your character's obstacles, which should be seemingly impossible, but not.

Within the conflict of the second act, the protagonist and the antagonist face off like two boxers in a ring. All of the actions taken by the protagonist in act two are the direct result of the goal that set the protagonist on his or her journey in the first act—cause and effect. Keep in mind, however, that the intensity of the obstacles and the conflict must match the intensity of the goal. This intensity will inevitably cause your characters to develop and change (or go through the character arc), which will become evident in the third act—the end of the journey and the end of the character arc.

Although act two has thus far been a series of conflicts and obstacles for the protagonist, something happens halfway through the second act that causes the protagonist to recommit to the goal. This event is the midpoint and it, too, advances the storyline, but in a different direction.

From the midpoint, the story really intensifies toward the second turning point, crisis, or what I call the low point. At this juncture, all seems lost for the protagonist—there appears to be no hope. The protagonist is at a crossroads and must make a critical decision, a final decision that will thrust him or her into the third act and to the conclusion. The low point quickens the pace of the remainder of the story (the third act).

Pace is an important factor in act two. Counting the events or beats in the story will help you determine whether you need to slow, maintain, or speed up the pace of your script. Switching between heavy and light scenes will also help pacing, as will switching between action and dialogue scenes. A good exercise for understanding pacing and applying it to your script is to compare an action-genre, high-concept script such as *Speed* or *The Italian Job* to a low-concept story script such as *House of Sand and Fog* or *Life as a House*. When you look through various well-written scripts, you will notice a pattern—every high or positive event is (or should be) followed by a low or negative event.

ACT III

You planted the seeds in act one and created a debt between you and the audience. Now it's the time to pay off your debt. In act three, your main character's story and all of the subplots should be resolved. In addition, the story question should be answered in the highest climactic and dramatic point of the story. The third act may foreshadow a future story and conflict, but the story you told for the past 90 pages must be settled.

Mechanically, the third act contains pivotal plot points such as the climax, resolution, and denouement. If your screenplay is low concept, the ending may be ambiguous. But beware, ambiguity is rarely acceptable for big Hollywood blockbusters, which tend toward happy, neat, and tidy endings. Hollywood blockbuster endings are often ridiculed as being pure entertainment—but what's wrong with that? After all, don't most audience members go to the movies for entertainment? Just make sure your ending fits your concept.

Whatever you do, whether your script is low concept or high concept, never end your story with *deus ex machina*, Latin for "god out of the machine." In many plays written in ancient Greece and Rome, the gods would come out of nowhere and resolve all the conflict for the characters at the end. If you are having trouble understanding *deus ex machina*, watch the movie *Dodgeball*. There's a great parody on the concept at the end (read what's on the treasure chest). From this example, you will surely understand *deus ex machina* and why it's so cheesy in a screenplay.

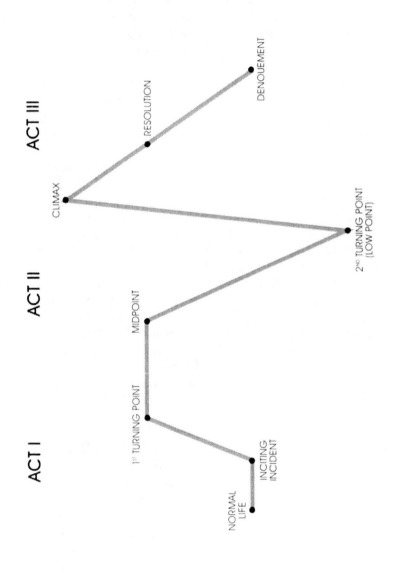

Almost immediately after your main character's low point in act two, he or she will face the climax. At the climax, your character's goal is on the line—it's the final showdown. The protagonist has walked the plank and is standing on the edge. What will the protagonist do? The climax is the final conflict where the action is the most intense . . . it is where the character makes his or her final decision, which solves the story problem.

The outcome of the climax, positive or negative, moves the story to its resolution. The resolution reveals the effect of the climax and answers the hovering story question. In addition, the resolution reveals the theme or author's attitude toward the protagonist and the protagonist's goal. Because the climax is the last conflict of the script, the resolution should be extremely close to the end of the act.

But the resolution cannot be the end, because the audience still needs to experience a sense of closure and return to the world of reality. It's like the end of a rollercoaster ride. The ride doesn't end immediately after a steep drop—that would be too sudden for the riders. Instead, the rollercoaster slows its speed and follows a straight line back to the boarding station and the riders disembark, exhilarated. Or, in the age of Prozac®, a patient wouldn't (or shouldn't) stop taking the pill cold turkey: he or she must be weaned off it slowly. The ride back to the boarding station or the weaning stage of prescription drugs is comparable to the denouement plot point of the third act. The denouement is the result of the resolution—what life is like for the character(s) after the challenge has been completed and the goal has or has not been achieved. The audience wants to know what happened to the character. If Peter Jackson had ended *The Return of the King* immediately after the One Ring was destroyed in the fires of Mount Doom, we, the audience would never know how the destruction of the ring actually affected all those we followed during the 557-minute journey. Just remember that the denouement is for the audience. Likewise, the denouement is most often used as a means to emotionally and psychologically release the audience from the ride they just experienced. It comes very soon after the climax and resolution, quickly ending the story.

Although third acts are short and your audience's attention span has been challenged by this point, you should not allow yourself to have a shortened attention span when it comes to the third act. Your characters did not take you on a journey and then just drop you. Likewise, you should not take your audience on a journey just to drop them when it matters most. The third act is about respect—respecting your characters and respecting your audience.

Believability

I am very strict in my client analyses when it comes to believability. Even one element of unbelievability can ruin the realistic aspects of the script. However, I understand that believability is built around odds rather than definitively. Aristotle said, "Dramatic effect derives from what is probable, and not from what is possible."

Depending on the genre, setting, and time of the story, some circumstances may be more believable and acceptable than others for the audience. But instead of concerning yourself with what is probable (which seems to indicate a sense of certainty, logic, and guarantee), focus on what is plausible for the type of story you have written, which implies greater imagination, possibility, and creativity within the realm of the story world.

Subplots

Subplots interweave throughout act two with the protagonist and the protagonist's goal. Subplots serve many purposes— comic relief, romance, dramatic effect, and pure entertainment, to name just a few. As your script's doctor, be aware that subplots can confuse the genre of your script, especially in comedies and romantic comedies. *How to Lose a Guy in Ten Days* is a romantic comedy because the romance and relationship between Ben and Andie is the main focus of the story. In *Billy Madison*, Billy is in love with Veronica; however, that love interest is not the main goal for Billy, so the movie is categorized as a comedy with a romantic subplot.

Subplots entangle themselves with the theme of the story and represent the theme. For instance, in *The Lord of the Rings* trilogy, each subplot character, in the fellowship and beyond, represents the theme, "No matter how small a role we play, it all makes a huge difference in the outcome of things"; or, as Galadriel says, "Even the smallest person can change the course of the future."

One of the main reasons for subplots is to reveal the three-dimensionality of the characters. Subplots are like the meditation, self-awareness side of body wellness—they allow insights into true character—whereas the intense, fast-paced, aerobic side of body wellness can be compared to the main story plot.

In addition to revealing character, subplots also aid in avoiding predictability in the story, which is why the rewriter should aim to incorporate between one and five subplots. *The Lord of the Rings* has numerous subplots . . . far too many to discuss in this book, but here are a few:

1. Merry, Pippin, and the Ents (*The Two Towers*)
2. Aragorn, Gimli, and Legolas (*Fellowship of the Ring, The Two Towers*, and *The Return of the King*)
3. Aragorn and Éowyn (*The Two Towers* and *The Return of the King*)
4. Aragorn and Arwen (*Fellowship of the Ring, The Two Towers*, and *The Return of the King*)
5. Boromir, Faramir, and the Steward of Gondor (*The Return of the King*)
6. Arwen, Elrond, and the sailing to the Undying Lands (*Fellowship of the Ring, The Two Towers*, and *The Return of the King*)

All of these subplots interweave with Frodo's journey to destroy the One Ring, the main plotline of all three films.

Because the subplots are interwoven into the main plot, it is inevitable that their structure will parallel the structure of the main plot. In other words, subplots, like the main plot, have a beginning, middle, and end, along with their own turning points.

Like the main plot, the subplot must have structure, but it should never overshadow the main plot. Otherwise, you risk confusing the audience.

Treatment for Structure and Plot Problems

Much like the treatment for premise and theme problems, completely understanding structure and plot is the number one thing a rewriter can do to refine these parts of a script. Again, there is no better way to begin to understand structure and plot than to assess the structure and plot of an already successful film—the film must have done well at the box office for a reason. And the reason for the success of these films is based on one or both of these factors: character and plot.

Here is what you should do to refine your script's structure and plot:

1. Refer to the already produced film you chose to evaluate in chapter 4.
2. Assess the movie's conflict. How is it introduced in act one? How is it handled throughout the story, especially in act two? How is it resolved in act three?
3. Given the blank heartbeat plot chart (on the next page), follow along with the movie and fill in the plot points as you see them. The more times you watch the particular film and the more films in general you watch, the easier it will be to fill in the chart.
4. After watching the films and plotting them out, go ahead and plot your own story. By doing so, you will be able to see any holes and weaknesses in your script that you will need to refine.

At UCLA, there were many instances when I had to evaluate and apply the structure and plot of a particular film—two in particular that come to mind are *The Full Monty* and *Dave*. This exercise is not an easy task and has the potential to be overwhelming.

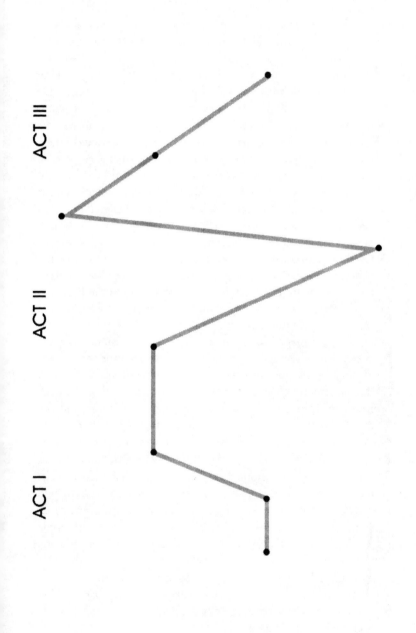

ACT I   ACT II   ACT III

If you don't feel comfortable evaluating the structure and plot of a film right away, children's books accomplish the same goal and work quite well because of their simplicity. Professor Jim Levi introduced my class to basic structure and plot by making us read the children's book *Pancakes for Breakfast* by Tomie De Paola. The book's premise is simple: An old woman wants to make herself pancakes for breakfast. Comparing the story in the book to the three-act structure of a screenplay, it would follow the plot heartbeat chart like this: An old woman wakes up from her slumber along with her dog and cat (normal life). The old woman craves pancakes for breakfast (inciting incident). So, the old woman grabs her cookbook to check the ingredients and decides to make the pancakes (first act turning point and the end of act one). In act two of *Pancakes for Breakfast*, the old woman is faced with many obstacles and conflict while trying to make her pancakes. First, she discovers that she is out of eggs and needs to retrieve some from the hen house. Then she's out of milk, so she braves the cold and snowy walk to the barn to milk the cow. After a couple of hours churning butter, the old woman is tiring. However, she completes the churning and envisions her pancakes, reaffirming what her hard work has been for and recommitting to her goal of making the pancakes (midpoint). As if things couldn't get worse, the old woman realizes she doesn't have any syrup to top her pancakes when they are completed. So, the old woman makes her way into town and buys some syrup from a man selling it. On the way home, the old woman envisions her pancakes once again—all seems wonderful until the old woman steps in her front door and finds her dog and cat making a mess with the ingredients she worked so hard to pull together (low point/second turning point). At this point, all seems lost . . . until the old woman senses a wonderful aroma coming from her neighbor's house (climax). The old woman treks across the snow, invites herself in, and sits down at the table with pancakes in front of her (resolution). At home, the old woman rests in her rocking chair next to the fireplace with her hands on her belly, satisfied—the dog and cat are sleeping on the floor by her feet (denouement).

Besides the structure and plot of *Pancakes for Breakfast*, the book contains many other similarities to screenplays in general.

Pancakes for Breakfast has a clear premise that can be summed up in this logline: An old woman who wants to eat pancakes for breakfast will stop at nothing to get them.

The theme of the book surfaces at the end of the story, much like the theme of a screenplay should. In fact, the theme blatantly appears on an embroidered wall hanging on the last page of the book; it says, "If at first you don't succeed, try, try, again." Ironically, the stitched words of the theme hanging on the wall are the only words in the entire 28-page story. This means that De Paola did a great job at showing the story rather than telling it ... and it's a book! Like *Pancakes for Breakfast*, screenplays should always show instead of tell, using as little dialogue as possible.

Moreover, each page of *Pancakes for Breakfast* can be compared to an effectively structured scene of a screenplay. Each page or scene in the book leaves the old woman seemingly farther away from the scene goal, while always moving her closer to the overall story goal—each scene (or page, in this case) constantly moves the story forward.

As far as characters, the old woman is obviously the protagonist, the kitchen is her antagonist, and there is even a supporting cast—the dog and the cat.

In addition to previous plot refinement alternatives, you may refine your plot through these steps as well:

- Figure out where your overall story begins, making sure it doesn't start too soon. Remember, like a scene, you want it to start at the latest point possible.
- Figure out the ending. If you know where you are going, it will be easier to figure out exactly how to get there.
- Employ the process of elimination. Put your scenes on index cards or, my personal favorite, on Post-it® notes, and put them into the second act. You are now filling out the middle of your story. Make sure you have a midpoint, second turning point, climax, resolution, and denouement, along with conflict and obstacles. If you find something missing,

go back to your deleted scenes file (see chapter 3) and see if the missing piece is there. If not, think back to what makes a scene and create something that fills the void.

- Write a treatment, beat by beat. Typically, a screenwriter prepares a treatment when he or she starts writing a script, but it also serves as a useful tool for assessing what you have already written and want to refine.

CHAPTER 7

Operation Dialogue

"Fasten your seatbelts, it's going to be a bumpy night."
—Bette Davis,
All About Eve, 1950

Symptoms of Dialogue Problems

- Doesn't fit the character
- Generic
- Contains clichés
- Overly expository
- Emotionless
- Unmotivated
- No story progression
- Not fluid
- Boring

DIALOGUE IS ONE OF THE HARDEST aspects of a script to write but one of the easiest to refine. If the dialogue doesn't achieve what it is supposed to, you must simply cut it. Dialogue serves many purposes in a script—moving the story forward, portraying character, revealing past information, setting the tone of the story, etc. Dialogue should be used sparingly in a script, preserving a film's visual appeal. Dialogue, although it reveals character and moves the story forward, should come second to action, which accomplishes the same goals but does so cinematically instead of narratively. Dialogue and action together are the meat of what makes the story move forward. However, action should contain the succulent juice of the story, while dialogue should follow a strict lean diet, avoiding protracted language and chitchat. In other words, dialogue should support the action and not be the main method for character revelation or story movement. Putting action before dialogue in importance ensures that the script's pace will remain upbeat and guarantees anticipation for each scene to follow. The audience will remember the action expressing an emotion more than the dialogue expressing an emotion. For example, although George Lucas is praised and revered as a filmmaker, his dialogue continues to undergo criticism. When I left the movie theater after seeing *Star Wars: Episode II - Attack of the Clones*, I immediately commented that most of the dialogue seemed cheesy, repetitive, and lacked subtlety. But, directly following that comment, I remarked to my friends how the use of certain looks and gestures between the characters (Anakin and Padmé, especially) seemed to redeem any weak dialogue. This demonstrates that nonverbal communication can be more effective and richer than dialogue. The same scenario is true for *Star Wars: Episode III - Revenge of the Sith*; one of the most poignant and emotionally moving scenes of the film contains no dialogue. As Padmé and Anakin gaze out separate windows, neither of them says anything, and the audience knows that Anakin has made the choice to turn to the dark side.

Dialogue is often the last element reviewed in a professional script analysis because, as Alfred Hitchcock said about writing a screenplay, "Build your screenplay first, then add dialogue." It may be difficult for you to decide where to begin to refine the dialogue in your script, especially when you are unclear about what your dialogue should accomplish within the story.

Dialogue should always open a door for the audience into the character's world, internally and externally. Dialogue should also reveal character aspects such as goal, motivation, back-story, history, setting, and believability. Dialogue, if executed properly, communicates necessary information about the story, inevitably moving the plot forward.

Great dialogue reveals itself when audience members leave the theater referencing lines of dialogue spoken by your engaging characters. That's why I quoted Bette Davis in *All about Eve* at the beginning of this chapter. The *All About Eve* quote is one of two references to a film older than 1980 in this book, and it demonstrates that good dialogue will stick around for a lifetime. It endures because of its curt delivery and simplicity.

As discussed in chapter 3, scenes mimic the mechanics of an entire screenplay through characters, goals, or conflict, all with the purpose of moving the story forward. Dialogue is no different; it too, should always move the story forward, along with revealing characters internally and externally and containing some amount of conflict. Good dialogue multitasks between characterization and exposition in the scene by means of balancing dialogue and action.

Although other forms of creative writing like plays and novels can contain longer bouts of dialogue, screenplays follow the rule of most written documents; that is, cut the fat and make them as short and to the point as possible. Although script dialogue should imitate the way real people speak, even the shortest of real-life dialogue can be made shorter. For example, "Um, yeah" can be shortened to "Yeah" unless the longer version is significant to the character and story. David Trottier calls script dialogue "edited speech." I like to say that screenplay dialogue goes through a filtration system. In today's technological society, dialogue should reflect the dialogue between real people during an instant messaging session. Think about it: it's short, to the point, and, unlike face-to-face exchange, you eliminate the "ums" and "ahs."

Good dialogue depends on the writer's complete knowledge of the characters—their goals and characterizations. Because you have already learned how to refine your characters to reflect your full understanding of them, you will be able to apply that knowledge toward the characters' dialogue so that it reflects their true personas as well. You must also know each character's goal and objective in order to create effective scenes, as discussed in chapters 3 and 5. Remember, when a person speaks, often he or she subconsciously allows his or her personality to surface.

Language Arts

Language should be right for the character and right for the setting in which the story takes place. The components of common speech are vocabulary, grammar, accent, slang/jargon, and rhythm. Dialogue is not always a true indicator of a human being's demeanor, much less a character's—that's why actions are so important; they prove true or false what is presented through dialogue, thus eliminating stereotypes. When I moved to Los Angeles from Minnesota (where I had lived all of my life), I can't count how many times my dialogue was picked apart. My vocabulary was different. I asked for "pop" instead of "soda" and my accent was ridiculed (unoriginally, I might add) for its heavy exaggeration of certain letters like "o" and the way I said "bag" (I still can't figure that one out). I guess I accented the "a," as in "ace", but it should be pronounced like a sheep does . . . "baaag." I didn't get it then and I still don't get it now. Oooh . . . yes . . . not . . . too . . . mention . . . the . . . rhythm . . . and . . . speed . . . of . . . my . . . speech. Apparently, these are all parts of my dialogue that scream: "Hey, this lady is from the Norte, yah den don'tcha know!"

Some language areas such as dialect and accent can be left up to the actor or actress playing the character, so you may simply indicate that the character has an accent. After that, however, do not attempt to use the accent or the dialect in your script. In addition, avoid slang whenever possible, because it dates a script.

Professional script analysts look hard for consistency when it comes to the language of a character because it is crucial for revealing character. Make sure that your characters always speak in the same accent, grammar, vocabulary, and rhythm throughout the entire story. Speaking of rhythm, the dialogue's rhythm affects the pacing of the story and should be paced like scenes—back and forth, high and low, long and short. Characters think and then speak and/or act as ideas come to mind—a stimulus/ reaction, whether the stimulus is visual or auditory. To help with the rhythm of your dialogue, remember that the last line of a scene's dialogue and the last line of a film's dialogue should be the strongest and most powerful and, therefore, memorable for the audience. A great example of ending dialogue is Yoda in *Star Wars: Episode Two - Attack of the Clones* when he says, "Begun, the Clone War has."

Although long speeches should be used sparingly, if they encompass good rhythm, they may work well. Look at repetitions in your story's dialogue, such as speaking something and then showing the same thing, along with the repetition of phrases, sentences, and words, such as names. Once you have introduced the character, don't keep mentioning his or her name unless it is called for by the scene. This is a common pitfall, especially because calling people by name is commonplace in society. A close friend of mine constantly states the name of the person to whom she is speaking. Granted, it is a good attention getter and in some ways creates a closer connection between the speakers, but the repetition can get very annoying, because it is simply not necessary. If something annoys you in real-life conversations, it will undoubtedly annoy your audience.

Subtext

The importance of having an ample amount of subtext in your script cannot be overstated. *Sub*text is (below the text) information in your dialogue that is implicit or metaphorical. Subtext is the underlying meaning of what a character says directly. What the character reveals through subtext tends to be about the character's subconscious need.

When you write subtext, you are avoiding the use of pronouns such as I, you, we, they, them, it, this, that, and those. Subtext is a participatory act for the audience, allowing them to decode the subtextual dialogue and thus creating a better understanding of the motivation of the character. If you, rewriter, were to express explicit dialogue at certain moments where subtext would be more effective, you are cheating the audience and in some ways insulting their intelligence. Although providing subtext may seem like teasing, cheating the audience out of subtext is worse, because audience members expect to engage intimately with the characters on the screen.

Exposition

Exposition is difficult to create because it only serves the audience. It includes all the information necessary for the audience to completely engage in and understand the story and characters. To prevent boredom, sift exposition into your story instead of pouring it out all at once. Expository information that is not essential to the story or to the audience's understanding of the story should be omitted during the refinement stage.

Exposition can be accomplished in various ways, including:

- *A narrator.* The narration is provided by the viewpoint character the writer has selected. This can be oral narration or written narration, as seen in the opening of the Star Wars trilogy and prequels.
- *Conflict.* Exposition can be concealed in conflict, thus cinematically manipulating the audience into believing they are not witnessing blatant exposition.
- *Visually.* In *The Garnet*, a copy of the *Los Angeles Times* is thrown onto the table, indicating the location, the time, and the major headline, showing and telling the audience about the governor's murder, which just happens to be the inciting incident.
- *Humor.* More specifically, the juxtaposition of humor and conflict.
- *Delay.* A very talented client of mine, Mark Kurasz, submitted a script to me that exhibited one of the best exposition delays I have seen. The script opened with the protagonist tearing up his small hometown with his bike, being very

mischievous. I really had to try to figure out why this character was so mischievous. The effect of this delay of exposition sparked my interest and I wanted to know more about the character. The screenwriter didn't leave me hanging, either—he revealed the character little by little, making sense of the character's actions in the beginning of the script. Delaying exposition sparks audience interest and participation.

- *Flashbacks and dream sequences.* Flashbacks and dream sequences should be used sparingly, because they are often used as a crutch. They also have the potential to make the movement and flow of the story come to a screeching halt for the reader and for the audience. The skilled screenwriter and rewriter is able to write and refine a flashback so that it brings the reader or audience into the past for necessary story information without interrupting the emotional experience they should be receiving from a forward-motioned story.

A flashback is a scene, and much like any other scene, it contains conflict. In addition, a flashback scene should also begin at the latest possible moment. The effectiveness of flashbacks and dream sequences depends on their length—keep them as short as possible—and whether they move the story forward.

Some script analysts view flashbacks and dream sequences as a "do not enter" zone. I choose to look at them as an "enter with caution" zone. I say this because, when I do have the pleasure of encountering a flashback or dream sequence that actually serves its purpose, it creates a "wow" factor that leaves me breathless. In addition, Mark Kurasz submitted a script to me entitled *Thicker than Water* that contained two such instances of breathtaking cinematic expression—one a flashback and one a dream sequence. The premise of *Thicker than Water* is: Three very different brothers bond together in an effort to destroy some of their town's most deadly secrets *and* people. Two of the brothers

(Garrett and Kid) both feel responsible for their mother's
death (which occurred before the current story started).
Let's take a look at the flashback and the dream sequence
in *Thicker than Water*. Then I'll discuss why the scenes
are so effective.

The dream sequence:

BLACK AND WHITE DREAM MONTAGE:
A very pregnant woman (late 30s) tumbles down
stairs. Rushed in ambulance. E.R. works fran-
tically to save her. Young Jack (forty) waits
nervously. Doctor enters. Bad news. At funeral,
Jack is flanked by his two sons: Cory (20) and
Garrett (10).
Hitchcock-like, fingers point at us as voices whis-
per: "you did it," "she's dead," "it's **you**," "**you**."
Kid wakes up and gets his bearings; Cadence
snores and an owl hoots, "**who**," "**who**."
The letter sticks out of Cadence's pocket. Kid
lifts it like a burglar and reads it. His face
transforms to "holy shit!"

The flashback:

BLACK AND WHITE FLASHBACK:

A ten-year-old Garrett pouts on the stairs with
Matchbox® cars. His very pregnant mother comes
up the steps.

                       COLLEEN
        (Irish Accent)
    Ah honey, ya don't have nothin' to worry
    about. Mommy's gonna have plenty of love
    for all three of her children.
        (still pouts)

```
You'll still be my favorite . . . I promise.
  (crosses her heart)
How about we get some ice cream?
  (Garrett glows)
Clean up your cars and I'll fetch me coat.
```

She heads up, and returns with her coat. Garrett waits below.

CLOSE on her foot as she steps on a Matchbox® car.
Garrett's face is horrified as Mommy tumbles, her lifeless body landing at his little Hush Puppies®.

The dream sequence clearly conveys to the audience that Kid blames himself for his mother's death since he was the one in the womb at the time—sort of a "If I wasn't conceived, this would have never happened" theory from Kid's point of view. Notice that Kid's dream sequence contains action, a sense of urgency, a quick pace—it is very participatory. The sequence is quick—in, out, and onto the next action of "the letter sticks out of Cadence's pocket. Kid lifts it like a burglar and reads it. His face transforms to 'holy shit.'" The transition from "it's you," "you," to the sound of an owl in real time saying "who, who" is also extremely well done.

By contrast, in the flashback, Garrett remembers his inter-pretation of how and why his mother died—clearly pegging himself as the cause (he left out his Matchbox® cars, so his mother tripped on them and fell down the stairs). Again, this flashback is effective because it is quick. The flashback visually provides the boy's age without needing to state it; it shows instead of tells. We, the audience, know that Garrett is very young because he plays with Matchbox® cars. The flashback appeals to the audience emotionally and creates a connection for them when Garrett watches his mother fall to her death. The scene is intense. The death is very dramatic, as it should be.

Despite all the other wonderful aspects of this flashback, my favorite is immediately at the beginning of the scene. How ironic it is that Colleen says to Garrett, "Ah honey, ya don't have nothin' to worry about." Worrying is all that Garrett has done for his entire life! Garrett has fretted over his belief that he caused his mother's death.

The two brothers, Kid and Garrett, have lived with guilt their whole lives and for most of the script. Audience members, knowing that both brothers hold such different views and knowing that they should not feel guilty, share their heartache.

Overall, the dream sequence and flashback in *Thicker than Water* are very effective because they compare and contrast with each other, along with revealing character.

The flashback and the dream sequence should be kept in the story because they are not used as a crutch and because they enhance the story by revealing the characters of Garrett, Kid, and, on some level, Colleen. They also reveal the characters' internal conflicts. They enhance the story instead of taking away from it.

Sometimes flashbacks can be more effective and acceptable if there is some provoking device before the scene that prompts the flashback, like a song, an object, a place, an image, and so on.

Again, sparingly relay exposition through dialogue. Its sole purpose is to expose necessary information, such as past experiences, feelings, and motivations to the audience (and only to the audience). But it should reveal information in a concealed manner. Unlike subtext, which serves the characters, the actors that portray those characters, and the audience members, exposition is only necessary for the audience so they can learn what the characters already know.

Use exposition in moderation to prevent audience boredom. Spice it up with comedy, delay it as long as possible (for instance, show a character's actions before his reasoning), provide it during a scene of conflict between the characters—a comedic, action, or love scene. Remember, exposition should never be the only goal of a scene, because it can only hold the audience's attention for so long. According to David Trottier, "about ninety-five percent of the flashbacks in unsold scripts doesn't [*sic*] work." Perhaps this is because their flashback scenes only offer exposition.

Treatment of Dialogue Problems

Like researching prototypes for characters, refining story dialogue so that it completely achieves what it should requires research on how people speak, what they say, and how they say it. You need to pay attention and listen. Your ultimate goal after the examination and refinement of your script's dialogue is to have your characters speak in a way that is accurate, understandable, and effective. By effective, I mean that the dialogue reveals character, reveals back-story information, moves the story forward, sets the tone, and evokes emotion.

After your dialogue research, apply what you have learned about scenes and characters by evaluating each scene in your screenplay to assess the need for dialogue refinement:

- Determine what is happening in the scene.
- Determine what each individual character wants in the scene and what (action) he or she will employ to achieve it. Know your characters' distinctions, their responses to various questions and situations.
- Determine what one character does not want revealed to another character.
- Determine whether words are necessary for the character to get what he or she wants or whether it can happen with a look or gesture.

Once you have applied your assessment and refined your dialogue as you feel appropriate, have someone (preferably an actor/actress) read it aloud. Hearing the script in a different voice than your own is an eye-opening experience. Many colleges have theater departments with actors who may be willing to help you. Or, if you don't have access to any actors, have friends or family members read the script aloud for you. Having someone read it aloud *after* you have revised it will help your proofreading as well; keep these people in mind when you complete your rewrite. Using your auditory skills and allowing your visual skills to rest will help you discover any parts of the dialogue that are still not working. You will be able to assess the rhythm, content, subtext, and overall tone of the dialogue in each scene.

PART III

Cosmetic Surgery

CHAPTER 8

What Genre Am I?
A Script's Identity Crisis

"Bad movies and bad company just don't mix."
—Therese Ribas

ALTHOUGH AUDIENCE EXPECTATIONS remain the same, today's audiences have a much different experience when going to the movie theater than the generations before them. First, the tickets cost a small fortune. And in the age of branding, audiences have to put up with endless preshow advertisements and even commercials. Now, besides nagging coughs, whispers, or even downright loud talking, audiences must try to block out the piercing sound of cell phones that seem to ring at key moments in the plot. Audiences do not need any more distractions or irritations to ruin the wonderful cinematic experience they are entitled to—especially the irritation of viewing a film that promised to deliver and failed.

Audience Experience

People love films because they are an emotional experience. Although different people want and expect different things from movies (depending on the viewer's age)—including motivation, education, challenge, or an alternate reality—the emotional experience puts audience members into theater seats.

To create a cinematically compelling script that will not only meet but also rise above the audience's expectations, you must completely understand the audience to whom your story will appeal. British drama critic Kenneth Burke calls this "understanding the psychology of the audience." In other words, understanding when to give the audience what they want and expect at the best dramatic point in the story.

Emotion is a universal human characteristic. American-made films affect audiences in foreign countries and, likewise, international films affect American audiences. The best films evoke emotions despite their original language because of what is shown rather than what is spoken.

For some, going to a movie is a personal and private venture. For others, it is a chance to experience the movie in the company of friends and share each other's experience. A close friend of mine will often go to movies by himself—matching his very independent personality. For him, it is personal time to escape reality and completely immerse himself in the lives and adventures of others.

I personally prefer to share my movie experience with friends and family, particularly with friends and family members who like to do the same. I like the discussions afterward, over a bite to eat. Being able to discuss a film signals dynamic audience participation. My friends and family get angry with me because I love to (according to them) overanalyze films. This enhances my viewing experience, but can often take away from or altogether ruin their experience.

The best time to go to a movie, particularly a sequel, prequel, or adapted film, is immediately after release, because this is when you can best observe audience experience and participation in the film. When asked about the audience's affect on an individual's movie experience in Tom Stempel's *American Audiences on Movies and Moviegoing*, Lizy Moromisato says, "When there is a bigger audience rooting for a particular character in the movie, laughing at a joke, in other words reacting to the movie along with you, one feels more involved with the movie."

Audience dynamics shift the longer a film stays in the theater. I saw each of *The Lord of the Rings* installments at least three times over the course of their extended theater stays. When each film was first released, my laughs, sobs, and anticipation blended into my surroundings and were shared by the entire theater, full of fans—people who knew all or most of the story already. As the crowds dwindled in the following weeks, I could tell the audience members were different. They had heard that the movies were great but knew very little about the complex story and, thus, were unable to appreciate all that the films had to offer. You could tell that this group had not read the books so they did not know the back-story. For example, Sam's mention of his father (the Gaffer) in *The Return of the King* was supposed to be funny, but few nonenthusiasts caught on.

Likewise, I saw *Star Wars: Episode II - Attack of the Clones* at least eleven times in the theater and, the longer it ran, the fewer laughs Obi-Wan Kenobi's scene received when he used "the force" on a customer in a bar selling "death sticks," mimicking a similar scene with the much older Obi-Wan Kenobi on Tatooine in *Star Wars: Episode IV - A New Hope*. Again, word of mouth reached those not completely knowledgeable about the complete back-story—or, in this case, future of the story.

Not every movie-going experience is positive for the audience in a large crowd. Earlier I mentioned that commercials and cell phones are supreme annoyances. To many, sharing a room with dozens of people is a huge distraction. Two particular run-ins I had with fellow audience members that I can remember involved a guy next to me taking notes of the film on his arm (conserving paper, I guess) and some teenage girls who giggled and professed their love for Orlando Bloom every time Legolas appeared in a scene in *The Lord of the Rings* . . . savages!

It's a shame that it had to come to this, but some hate the large crowds so much that they go to private screenings, smaller theaters, or simply wait to rent or buy the DVD, since DVDs are produced so rapidly now. My uncle often reminds me that in his youth he was a movie theater usher—keeping watch like a hawk over any disturbances that might disrupt an audience member's enjoyment. I like large audiences, but I wouldn't mind if theaters reinstated the usher position. It would probably mean an increase in ticket prices, but at least it would be for a justifiable reason. We expect audiences to put up with a lot for that one outstanding experience. But it's great when they are willing to see your film. Thus, your screenplay should be superb.

Audience Demographics

How much do you know about the people seated around you when you go to a movie? Probably not much, because it's not your job to know anything about them when you are *viewing* a movie. When you are writing and rewriting a film, however, it's your job to know as much about your audience as possible. When you are analyzing your script, you need to ask questions such as these:

Who really goes to movies?
Why do they go to the movies?
Will my story reach the audience it's meant to?

Now that you have asked yourself these questions, let's discuss the answers that you should arrive at if you are to be educated in audience demographics. So, who really goes to movies? Although men, women, and children all seek the emotional journey on the silver screen, men tend to embark on the journey more than women . . . specifically, men ages 18–34—a magical number series almost as important in the industry as Monday's box-office totals and the Neilsen ratings. Following the 18–34 males, the next key age group in cinematic attendance are women ages 18–24. During these ages, dating is prevalent and, because many of them don't have family responsibilities or established careers, many men and women during this stage of their lives have hefty disposable incomes. And what better way to spend time and money than at the movies?

You might be saying to yourself, "But I've seen people older than 34 at the movies!" Yes, men and women do go to the movies after the age of 34, so you needn't play paparazzi and snap pictures of these rarities to send to the *National Inquirer*. Older people are not a key demographic for industry professionals because there is a lower turnout of people over 34—their financial situations are different. Movies are a gamble. Unlike tangible purchases, film is subjective and members of the older age group want a guarantee that it's good before shelling out any money for it. A trailer may be enough to thrust an 18–34-year-old into the theater, but for the mature, it only sends them to the movie synopsis and review section of the newspaper. And even that isn't enough. They will most likely seek the reviews of their peers and then, just maybe, they will see the movie and avoid saying those dreaded words, "I'll rent it when it comes out." They don't want surprises; they want guarantees. When movie tickets in some places are $12.00 and higher, maybe guarantees are a good thing.

Will your movie script reach the audience it's meant to? Well, that depends on whether you are clear on the genre of your screenplay and if you know what types of audiences tend to follow that genre. Let's take a look at genre.

Genre

The term "genre" is used in both art and literature. Films are categorized based on certain essentials that encompass the particular genre. It is imperative that you determine the genre of your screenplay, because otherwise you have risked writing a story that may never find its audience.

Since it is a universal question in screenwriting, you should know its answer: When was the last time someone asked you the genre of your script? Now, how easy was it to tell that person the genre? If someone asks you what the genre is, you should be able to answer without a second thought. Drama. Comedy. Thriller. Amazingly, such a commonplace question is hard for many screenwriters to answer. Perhaps that's because there are so many genres and, if writers and executives are feeling particularly creative, they can even develop a new genre to fit their script. You, as a rewriter, must be able to explain your script's genre as quickly and efficiently as possible.

The first step in being able to convey your genre is to educate yourself about the different genre categories. To help, here's a list of fifteen typical genres; your script will most likely fall into one of them:

- *Action.* Characterized by the hero/heroine classically winning in the end. The action genre takes that character through a series of chases, explosions, and just about any special effect you can conceive. Action films are always made first in the industry, because action is the movie genre favored by the key demographic of moviegoers, the 18–34-year-old males. In addition, action films typically attract big-name celebrities like Vin Diesel, Mel Gibson, Nicholas Cage, John Travolta, and Arnold Schwarzenegger. Some examples of action films are *Lethal Weapon*, *Speed*, *Gone in Sixty Seconds*, *The Fast and the Furious*, and *The Italian Job*.
- *Adventure.* Action-packed films that usually have the main character going on some quest or exploration. Adventure films differ from the action genre in that they do not focus on violence, as the action genre tends to do. Some examples of adventure films are *Raiders of the Lost Ark*, *The Perfect Storm*, and *Pirates of the Caribbean*.
- *Comedy.* Comedies are produced purely to entertain, and they tend to capitalize on exaggeration. Comedy is a very large genre that can be divided into several subgenres, such as black comedy and slapstick comedy. Comedy, which is hard to do (or at least do well), sets its goal and plot around humor. Some examples of comedy films are *The Great Outdoors*, *Dumb and Dumber*, and *Meet the Parents*. Comedy can be intermingled with other genres; for example, with the romance genre: Romance + Comedy = Romantic

Comedy (*How to Lose a Guy in Ten Days*). A not so easy genre to cross with comedy is drama, but it can be done: Drama + Comedy = Dramedy (*Spanglish*).

- *Drama.* Along with comedy, drama is a very large genre characterized by tragedy and theme. Whereas I mentioned in chapter 3 that some scripts may not have a theme, that's not true for dramas. Dramas always have a message of some sort. Dramas are much easier to write than comedies and first-time screenwriters are more likely to attempt them. Maybe this happens because there is some sort of common knowledge or universal understanding and agreement on what suffering is, but what brings an individual joy and laughter is a bit more complex and different for everyone. Studios frequently release dramas in the last quarter of the year to coincide with Oscar considerations. Examples of drama films are *Driving Miss Daisy*, *Philadelphia*, *Forrest Gump*, *House of Sand and Fog*, *Cold Mountain*, and *The Notebook*.

- *Epic.* Epic films are grander in every way, their stories often based on a historical or mythic event. The budget for such productions is also grander. Examples of the epic film genre include: *Gandhi*, *Titanic*, *Gladiator*, and *Troy*. Like comedies, epics can be crossed with other genres. For instance: Epic + Science Fiction = *Star Wars: Episodes I–VI*; Epic + Fantasy = *The Lord of the Rings*; Epic + Western = *Dances with Wolves*.

- *Fantasy.* Films in the fantasy genre take place in imaginative or made-up settings. Fantasies usually have the protagonists going on heroic journeys where characteristics of the story involve creatures and situations that cross the line of reality. Examples of fantasy films include *The Neverending Story*, *Edward Scissorhands*, *The Lord of the Rings* trilogy, and the *Harry Potter* series.

- *Horror.* Horror films evoke fear from the audience members. The horror genre capitalizes on fear until it consumes the audience, resulting in an entertaining yet scary experience that often stays with them after they leave the theater. Example of horror films include *Poltergeist, Scream, The Mummy, The Ring,* and *Van Helsing.*

- *Mockumentary.* A very popular genre in contemporary society, a mockumentary is complete fiction offering the illusion that it is based on fact. The content of a mockumentary is exaggerated and farcical. It is filmed and delivered much like a documentary but is completely fictional. Examples of mockumentaries include *Best in Show* and *A Mighty Wind.*

- *Musicals.* Many classic films are musicals. Popular in the eighties, recent musical examples include such films as *Moulin Rouge* and *Chicago.* Musicals focus the story around elaborate songs and often incorporate dance. More examples of musicals include *Flashdance, Footloose,* and *Evita.*

- *Science Fiction.* The science fiction genre is similar to the fantasy genre in that both are imaginative. Sci-fi films are futuristic; often their locations are in outer space and on faraway planets and include advanced technology. Examples of science fiction genre films include *E.T. the Extra Terrestrial, The Abyss, Independence Day, Armageddon,* and *Star Wars: Episodes I–VI.*

- *Thriller.* The thriller genre requires a skilled screenwriter who is able to capitalize on suspense and create anticipation, anxiety, and tension for the viewer. The objective of thrillers is usually easy to explain and understand. The characters are dealing with a mystery or a dangerous situation. Examples of thrillers include *Fatal Attraction, Silence of the Lambs, Nick of Time, The Sixth Sense,* and *Cellular.*

- *War.* A war genre plot is based on some or all aspects of war. War films tend to take advantage of current social issues and may be used as propaganda. Examples of war films include *Platoon, Born on the Fourth of July, Courage Under Fire, Saving Private Ryan, Black Hawk Down,* and *Pearl Harbor.*

- *Western.* Westerns are a very old genre dating back to the beginning of film. Westerns are typically set in North America's

Western frontier and focus on the juxtaposition of nature and civilization. Examples of westerns include *Young Guns*, *Tombstone*, *Shanghai Noon*, *Open Range*, and *Unforgiven*.

Analysis of the Thriller Genre

One of my favorite genres is the thriller—any hybrid of it. Yes, I love them all—sci-fi thriller, action thriller, suspense thriller, and adventure thriller. For our discussion of genre conventions and characteristics, I will examine this genre and a film that perfectly exemplifies it, *Nick of Time*.

In general, the main goal of thrillers is to induce an adrenaline rush. Hence, thrillers are full of intensity and suspense. The goal is often very simple and clear, the stakes are extremely high, and the protagonist is placed in a menacing situation, keeping the audience on the edge of their seats.

Nick of Time is an action thriller with a political conspiracy backdrop. Here's the synopsis if you haven't read the script or seen the film: Accountant Gene Watson (played by Johnny Depp) arrives in Los Angeles with his six-year-old daughter. He is approached by two strangers who hold his daughter hostage and give him a nightmarish ultimatum: kill the governor, who's in town for a nearby rally, within 60 minutes or never again see his daughter alive.

An intense aspect of the thriller is that the problem cannot be solved through the usual means, like calling 911 or the police. Gene Watson also cannot seek the aid of the FBI or the governor's bodyguards. Gene is not only being constantly watched by the kidnappers, but he soon discovers that "everyone" is involved with the plot to kill the governor—including most of the governor's security team and even her husband.

Like any good thriller, the goal of *Nick of Time* is clear (to save his daughter by assassinating the governor), and the stakes are high if Gene fails (his daughter will be killed). This therefore, serves as adequate motivation.

The protagonist in a thriller typically embarks on a character arc where he or she is reactive and, by the middle and end, shifts to proactive, and this film is no different. Gene finally takes charge of the situation by getting help from a "Disabled War Vet" who shines shoes in the hotel where the rally is being held. With the help of the veteran and his hotel-insider savviness, Gene is able to reach the governor personally and explain the conspiracy against her.

Symbols used throughout the film, particularly clocks and watches, add to the theme and pace of *Nick of Time* and help create a sense of urgency for the audience. As mentioned previously, time is "running out" and this is clear to the audience, who participate in the events as they unfold and the intensity level increases.

The resolution of a thriller usually comes after a violent and action-filled climax. *Nick of Time* again is no exception. Prepared to kill the governor after specifically warning her of the conspiracy, Gene discovers that the walkie-talkies (the means by which the kidnappers communicate) do not work in the room where she is giving a speech. As he points the gun at the governor, Gene swiftly turns around, aims, and fires at one of the kidnappers. This leads to further violence and a chase, but inevitably and ironically leads to the bad guys being killed and Gene ultimately saving his daughter without killing the governor.

CHAPTER 9

Makeup vs. No Makeup:
The Hollywood Blockbuster or
Independent Masterpiece?

"Motion pictures are the art of the middle. Neither high nor lowbrow, they must integrate the desire for creativity with the needs of commerce to deliver a product for an audience almost as large as the population itself."

—Thom Taylor

YOU HAVE CROSSED OVER from the creative stage of your script to the logical and analytical stage. Now it's time to switch gears yet again. You will still be evaluating, but instead of assessing your creativeness, you will be assessing yet another aspect of screenwriting—the business aspect. This side of screenwriting is really just basic business—economics, marketing, and sales.

There's a lot of pressure on the studio executives and producers who make the decisions to put a script into production—their jobs are at stake. Unless your script is perfect and contains every element that makes a script marketable in Tinseltown, neither you nor anyone else will be viewing your film on the silver screen. So, during the analyzing and rewriting process, you must also assess your script's market potential and refine it as necessary to suit the needs of the industry.

When your script is ready for submission—in other words, you have completely evaluated and refined its creative parts—two possible markets await it: Hollywood or the independent market. Both markets require different levels of commercial appeal and you should learn about both so that you can make the proper script adjustments during the rewriting process.

As do Hollywood's story analysts, studio executives and marketing teams need to know what makes a script salable. If you are truly to be your own script doctor, you too must know what elements are required of your screenplay so that you and the industry can make as much money from it as possible.

The Hollywood Blockbuster–bound Screenplay

Synonymous with blockbuster are the words "epic," "chartbuster," and "runaway success." In other words, a blockbuster film is "big" in every aspect—from the concept to the box office. A Hollywood blockbuster can cost a studio $10 million alone for media hype such as mugs, rides, and games to get the audience's attention.

The number one goal of a Hollywood blockbuster script is to attract a large audience. Why? Because the average cost for a studio producing a blockbuster is about $80 million—up 100 percent from 1999. Studios and producers want to be sure they turn a profit, and a film has to bring in three times the budget in order to turn a profit.

Although Monday's box office results of the opening weekend for a movie are crucial, the second weekend and return customers are the true proof of a movie's success.

Hollywood blockbusters must appeal to a mass audience. Studios try to guarantee their big movies are blockbusters by casting well-known actors. Actors who make about $20 million per movie are costly but crucial for audience appeal. Having a well-known actor or actress somewhat guarantees a successful opening weekend, despite what may happen after the reviews come out. For instance, although she appreciates movies in general, my mother prefers movies with actors such as Brad Pitt, Viggo Mortensen, and Jennifer Aniston, and she goes to see them as soon as their movies come out.

A Hollywood blockbuster-bound script should be based on the usual three-act structure, but all the individual elements—character, plot, dialogue, action, visuals, and concept—should be grandiose. A blockbuster should also blatantly display the distinct characteristics of its specific genre and give the audience what it has come to expect. If your script contains these characteristics, it's a blockbuster.

Let's look at the top five grossing films for the last four years. Notice that they all include the commercial elements studio executives are looking for to attract the largest possible audience.

- *2004. Shrek 2*; *Spider-Man 2*; *The Passion of the Christ*; *Meet the Fockers*; *The Incredibles.*
- *2003. The Lord of the Rings: Return of the King*; *Finding Nemo*; *Pirates of the Caribbean: The Curse of the Black Pearl*; *The Matrix Reloaded*; *Bruce Almighty.*
- *2002. Spider-Man*; *The Lord of the Rings: The Two Towers*; *Star Wars: Episode II - Attack of the Clones*; *Harry Potter and the Chamber of Secrets*; *My Big Fat Greek Wedding.*
- *2001. Harry Potter and the Sorcerer's Stone*; *The Lord of the Rings: The Fellowship of the Ring*; *Shrek*; *Monsters, Inc.*; *Rush Hour 2.*

Large studios like Paramount, Universal, Sony Pictures, Warner Brothers, and Disney are the ones that typically produce blockbusters. Moreover, many of the major studios have several niche genre subdivisions and have distribution deals with independent production companies. Studios are known for buying spec scripts from proven successful screenwriters or contracting with well-known writers. This approach increases their odds for success more than taking a chance on an unknown screenwriter.

Don't get me wrong, tapping into the Hollywood blockbuster market is not impossible. However, another market should not be overlooked: the independent script market.

The Independent-bound Screenplay

The independent world is a great place for the beginning writer to break into the film industry and make a name for him- or herself. Just take Steven Soderbergh, for example, whose *Sex, Lies, and Videotape* won at Sundance and Cannes in 1989. The independent filmmaking industry is known for taking more risks than the big studios—whether those risks are on writers, unknown actors, actresses, and directors, and/or on original, "noncommercial" concepts and stories.

Independent or indie films usually are very low budget and suffer from intense time restraints. The script quickly passes through the development stage and into production, unlike the Hollywood blockbuster. This does not mean that quality is compromised. *The Full Monty*, for example, was made for about $5 million and managed to gross over $200 million

It is evident to me from my exposure to the indie world that the critical components of an independent screenplay are the same as a script submitted to a large studio. They include the premise, the story, and the timing of the submission.

On the other hand, I have found two distinct differences in the requirements of each marketplace. First, large studios are quite concerned about "packaging" (the actors/actresses attached to a script) whereas indies are all about the writer and/or the filmmaker and embrace these artists' participation. Second, in large studios, the success of a particular film benefits the executive who decided to make it; the writer has little or nothing to do with the script after it is sold, but this is not true with indies.

In general, independent scripts tend to be more subdued, dramatic, and character driven. In addition, the independent industry has few set rules or guidelines because independent producers have no studio deals—they are, as their *independent* title implies, on their own.

To finance independent films, producers seek the help of studios, independent financing companies, and investors. Many actors and actresses own their own production companies and, since it is imperative to get actors and actresses interested in your script, you should find out who is signing deals.

As mentioned before, the structure of the independent-bound screenplay is important but, in general, the independent film industry is more open to unusual approaches—be it premise, theme, execution, characters, or dialogue. I once had a client whose script was absolutely brilliant and very unique in style as far as character and execution. His script should have been sent to the Sundance Institute or to another independent outlet. Unfortunately, the script was linear, no peaks and valleys, and it lacked a definitive three-act structure. Remember, although it is not as grand as a blockbuster, the structure of an independent script must still follow the proven three-act structure.

The Screenplay Market

It is not enough to write a screenplay that you hope a buyer will find commercial—you should know that the buyer will find it commercial. That means you must fully educate yourself in the business of screenwriting. It is true that you find an agent because agents are paid to know the business. But that's not enough.

To understand the industry as well as or better than your agent allows you to compete successfully against the many others in your field. When I came up with the idea to write this book, one of my first steps was to analyze the market and see if there was a need or desire for my idea. After that, I researched publishers to determine which ones published books for my target audience. If I had queried publishers that didn't publish my genre, I risked looking like an amateur and would have wasted a lot of time and money, both the publisher's and mine. A script's market is no different, but you need to know which studios buy and produce what you are selling, both genre and budget. Warner Brothers, for instance, is notorious for going big or not at all. If your script is a character drama and low concept, don't bother pitching it to Warner Brothers.

Great scripts are the result of the writer's passion. A brilliant script makes it easier to attach elements. When it comes down to it, the main thing that should sell a script is the script itself. Unfortunately, because the film industry runs on fear, sometimes the decision to buy or pass on a script isn't actually based on the script at all. Studio execs spend too much time analyzing and not enough time following their intuitions. The result? A lot of missed opportunities. But their wariness is understandable, because the studio exec's job is on the line much of the time. If a studio executive gives the green light to a film that bombs, there's a good chance that his or her job will be gone. The future of a company's success depends on the decisions made by its execs. Studio executives may be the most powerful people in the film industry, but I don't envy them.

The film industry in general is a gamble. No one ever really knows what will sell. I'm not a stock-market guru, but I do know that you shouldn't put all your eggs in one basket. No good businessperson would get involved in show business. Although all businesses balance logic and risk, the film industry is extremely risky for an entity that has to do so much just to make a profit or, heaven forbid, just break even. One area that film industry executives have in common with other business people is their concern and focus on finances. Businessmen and women in the film industry fret and try to ensure the best return on their shareholders' investments. Despite the fear the execs and the studios run on, they are always looking for good stories. Just try walking around a studio lot with a blank set of pages that resembles a script and see how many inquiries you receive about what you are carrying. Studios want good scripts and are constantly on the lookout for them.

Studios make movies in a certain order, depending on target audience. Action movies tend to be made first, because they target the number one theatergoers—the 18–34-year-old males we discussed in chapter 8. After action films, studios make comedies. Then come thrillers or psychological dramas. Currently, thriller and horror films are extremely popular, exemplified by the releases of *The Interpreter*, *The Ring 2*, *The Amityville*

Horror, *White Noise*, *Boogeyman*, *House of Wax*, *Cursed*, and *Dominion: Prequel to the Exorcist*. Although most first-time screenwriters typically write pure dramas, dramas are lower on the totem pole of production.

Whatever the genre, the market today revolves around branding the product (the film)—drilling it into the heads of consumers everywhere, repeating it over and over and over again until you get the picture (no pun intended) and the studio or production company gets results. The studios try to get consumers to see their movies through toys, video games, fast-food promotions, amusement park rides, and even entire amusement parks. Branding the film into the heads of the audience makes payday grand at the studios. In the weeks before the release of *Star Wars: Episode III - Revenge of the Sith*, I could open up just about any store advertisement in the local newspaper and find all kinds of *Star Wars* merchandise—action figures, games, even potato chips. These merchandise ads are an attempt to build anticipation and raise awareness of the film—to capitalize fully on the *Star Wars* empire.

The Spec Screenplay Market

There are two ways to sell a screenplay in Hollywood. One is to be hired by a studio or production company to write the screenplay for whatever project it is that they have in mind—an idea, an adaptation, or a rewrite. A screenwriter hired to write a screenplay based on a specific project typically is already successful.

The second way is to sell a "spec" script. A spec script is a script written by an independent or freelance writer solely on the speculation that it will be sold. The spec script is read and bought based on its ability to appeal to a wide audience. Past film successes and failures are what industry professionals use in order to determine what is commercial and what will continue to appeal to mass audiences. Many writers prefer to write on speculation, because it typically pays considerably better than contract jobs and there are usually no restrictions placed on their creativity.

In the early nineties, after the Writer's Guild of America strike of 1988, the spec market boomed. Before the strike, there were very few scripts sold on spec. Instead, studios or production companies contracted with writers for specific projects. But writers under contract during the strike became inpatient and began to write original scripts on speculation. As studios became desperate, prices paid for spec scripts soared.

The spec market has changed considerably throughout the years. Golden retrievers (people who search for scripts) used to buy what they personally liked, often based on a premise alone. While many scripts are still bought based solely on their ideas, the spec market has now shifted; buyers are more concerned with the package and what elements are attached to it.

The spec script market used to be a screenwriter's haven—an endless array of opportunities for both the experienced and the inexperienced to sell their screenplays. As I write this book, it appears that the spec market is suffering. We live in a corporate world, one that has expanded into the film industry. Corporate consolidation has obliterated some of the major studios, such as MGM (bought out by Sony and not currently buying material) and Miramax and Dimension (which are being subsumed more and more by their parent company, Disney). These consolidations make it difficult for other studios to buy and produce the volumes of spec scripts that they have bought and produced in the past. The remaining studios are paying significantly less for scripts. Ten years ago, a spec script would easily sell for half a million to a million dollars. Now, the paycheck for spec sales hovers between $100,000 and $300,000.

The effects of corporate consolidation run very deep. In an article entitled "The Death of the Script Market," posted in the January/February 2005 issue of *Creative Screenwriting*, Julien Thuan speaks of the competition that has occurred because of the loss of major studios. Thuan says, "That affects the level of difficulty of selling material, but it also affects how difficult it is to actually break in writers or directors because you don't have as many options." Another effect of corporate consolidation appears to be that buyers are only buying scripts that reflect what has already turned a profit in theaters. That means many studios are dipping into their archives, producing remakes and sequels. Studios are also buying adaptations such as novels, TV series, and comic books, because they are less risky. Currently, remakes and sequels are popular in the theaters; *War of the Worlds* is one example. Peter Jackson's reproduction of *King Kong* and the third of installment of *Shrek* are others. Although it might be safer for studios to produce remakes and sequels, audiences will catch on to this cautionary buying technique and may even resent the industry for the insult. Sequels and remakes have carried the "lack of originality" stigma for years.

The current situation of the spec script market is bad news for some and good news for others, particularly if you are an inexperienced writer trying to break into the business and do not mind selling your baby in the $100,000 to $300,000 range. Don't forget the independent film industry, either. It's a trade-off for all screenwriters, experienced or inexperienced. You may be paid less at times, but you'll have more job security—there will always be a need for scripts. No script means no film.

Although I have described the situation at the time of this writing, industry trends are very much cyclical and another shift, coming quickly in a positive direction, is quite possible. Moreover, buyers will come and buyers will go, and then they will come again. Although they are not buying the volumes they once did, buyers are still buying. All buyers need material to produce because, again, without screenplays, there are no movies. The spec scripts being bought today still need to have clear and commercial concepts and well-written stories. The only difference is that they need to be better than good—they need to be great.

The Process of Selling a Screenplay

Your ultimate goal in writing and perfecting your script is it to sell it. The process of selling a screenplay is much like a track meet—as much as track may seem like an individual sport, the time of each individual athlete is calculated for the total score and determines whether an athlete's team wins or loses. Getting a screenplay sold and produced is a collaboration between the writer(s), studio executives, producers, directors, marketers, actors, and many more people that you may or may not ever meet.

The first step in selling a screenplay is basic sales knowledge: sell the product (in this case, the script) when the buyers are buying. So, logically, the next step is finding which people are buying and getting them excited about what you are selling. You want to target buyers in the major studios, (Disney, Warner Brothers, Universal, etc.) or buyers for independent production companies.

Getting past the studio reader or the studio story analyst is your next hurdle. These people are the gatekeepers, and over 90 percent of the scripts they read will not be checked "pass." Between the story analysts and the marketing departments, they are looking for scripts that will most resonate with the audience.

The process of selling a script parallels the intensity that builds in the script's story plot. Follow me on this:

- You, the writer, get this magnificent, commercial idea for a screenplay (back-story).
- From the idea, you write, refine, and finish your screenplay (inciting incident).
- You finish the story and now need to sell the script or get an agent to sell the script for you (first turning point).
- You or your agent pitches it to a development executive, who then decides to show it to a producer (obstacle).
- The producer pitches the script to the studio executives, who fortunately decide to buy the script (obstacle and midpoint).
- Your script goes into development until it is or isn't greenlighted by the president of the studio (second turning point).
- If your script gets the green light, the final sell comes to the audience that has to view your story—will they emotionally connect with it like they should, or not? (climax and resolution).

You need to know the estimated budget of the potential movie you have written, since this will ultimately affect the buying of your script. The more expensive the script is, the more difficult it will be to sell. Many factors affect the budget of a film, particularly the above-the-line people and the below-the-line people, the special effects, and the story's setting or location. In Hollywood, there is an imaginary line between the creative or above-the-line talent (actors, actresses, producers, directors, and, yes, even writers) and the hands-on production staff or below-the-line talent (production manager, editors, cinematographer, and so on). Generally, this distinction can be compared to white-collar workers vs. blue-collar workers, a pecking order of the people that get a film made—even though all are equally important in the production and success of a film.

Below-the-line people significantly affect on the cost of making a film. Comedies are cheaper to make because the below-the-line people are cheaper to employ. In other words, you need to be aware of the technical and special effects aspects of your script, since below-the-line people will be implementing them.

In addition, be wary of having characters in your script that require casting children to play the roles. Because of strict child labor laws, the casting of children in films significantly raises the budget, so much so that casting directors will often select people to play roles who look younger than they really are. This tactic is very often used in television; for example, most of the actors in *Beverly Hills 90210* and *Dawson's Creek* were older in real life than the teenyboppers they played on the shows. Animals are also very expensive to have in film. So, unless your story depends on the casting of children or animals, I would highly suggest not including them in the script.

Special visual effects also greatly increase a budget, as do special locations for shooting. Be aware of these factors in your script. Without compromising the story, perhaps you may be able to change the setting of the story to a location that may be less expensive for the studio or production company to shoot.

Trends

Although you shouldn't rely only on trends to ensure the success of your script, it is important to know what's hot in the market, where it has been hot, and where the heat is going. Many professionals say you shouldn't write a script that doesn't match what's selling in the present market. I don't believe this to be true. You should always write what you are passionate about and, if it's not what's selling today, finish it and wait, because it will become hot at some point. Trends are cyclical; what goes around really does come around. If you are knowledgeable about trends, you automatically put yourself ahead of the competition.

In addition to knowing current trends when you finish your script, you should also have an idea of where the trends are headed, because from the time you finish a script until the time that you potentially see it on the silver screen usually takes two to three years. So if you want to time the marketing of your script properly, you need to know the past, present, and future of trends.

I encourage you to investigate trends. When gamblers go to casinos, they spend money. When skillful gamblers go to the casino, they also spend money, but they spend it in the areas that have the best odds of winning based on the research they have gathered beforehand. These knowledgeable gamblers still may lose, but they are less likely to lose than those who choose not to educate themselves. The same idea applies to trends and the writing of screenplays.

You must learn how to catch and surf the wave of trends. Surfing in the literal sense is very difficult. Living in southern California, I have attempted the sport. It takes many tries just to get up on the board and, when you finally do, you will probably cross in front of someone who will undoubtedly be frustrated and irritated with you. In addition, you will occasionally encounter dangers in the water, such as sharks. But when you finally do catch that wave and maneuver yourself over it (taking complete advantage of it), you will experience one exhilarating ride and have the satisfaction of controlling the board over something that is trying hard to resist you. Surfing is an excellent metaphor for how to catch and ride film industry trends. Know what has been produced, what is in theaters, and what is in production.

As Hollywood follows trends, so should you. Moreover, one successful film creates the opportunity for another. You should not look negatively on the success of your fellow screenwriters, because their success has opened the door for you. Just take a look at *Gladiator*. After that movie was made, *Troy* followed, then *Alexander*, and *Kingdom of Heaven* after that. Or look at all of the war movies made after *Saving Private Ryan*—*Black Hawk Down*, *Pearl Harbor*, and *Windtalkers*. Hollywood loves to capitalize on a trend, which is why I cannot emphasize enough the importance of becoming knowledgeable about this area of the business.

As easy as it is to recognize a Hollywood trend, it is just as easy to recognize the end of one. When spoof movies come out, such as *Scary Movie*, it's pretty much the nail in the coffin. Since actors and actresses have the power to green-light a project, watch for actor and actress trends as well as movie trends. Scripts become movies about three years from the time of their purchase. So look for stars of the future like Scarlett Johanssen, Hayden Christensen, Katie Holmes, Naomi Watts, and Orlando Bloom. Knowing actor and actress trends make you a savvy insider.

Trends constantly change because the desires and tastes of audiences are constantly changing. To best assess what will be a moneymaking film, producers and studios look not only to audience test-marketing and computerized projections, but also at concepts that have proven successful with audiences in the past. Trends also capitalize on current events. More or less, they have impeccable timing and tend to reflect the mood of society. During wartime, audiences look for escapist films—nothing too heavy to add to the heartache of war. Audiences are looking for superheroes or heroines who seem to save the day and make the world and the lives of the characters better. Audiences want to escape into the characters' lives—a world they wish existed in reality.

If a script similar to yours is in development or production, it is not likely that your script will sell at that moment. But that doesn't mean you should dump your script. That's why understanding trends and knowing what's hot now is so important. What's hot today will be hot again some day. So, finish your script and wait a while for your next opportunity to submit it. When the trend finally comes around again, don't hesitate for a second. In the meantime, begin writing another story—never put your creativity on hold for trends.

Making Your Script Commercial

It is crucial to have a plan when putting your script on the market. You need to research what is being bought and who is buying it in order to assess how to best market your product (the script). The market is tough and the competition fierce, so you need a marketing plan that is clear and precise.

In marketing, no matter what product or service you want to sell, the selling guidelines are: find, target, attack.

First, you want to find the areas of the market in which your product or service would best fit. Your product or service should be similar to those already sold within the market while maintaining the originality that separates you and your product or service from the rest.

Next, you want to identify or target the audience to whom you want to sell the product or service.

The final guide line is your plan of attack, based on the needs of the potential buyers. The plan of attack includes all of the tactics you use in your attempt to reach the buyers; for example, query letters or phone calls and luncheons. In many instances, I have had to write business letters about what I was selling. When I started the business Fourth Wall Coverage, I researched who my target audience would be and ended up writing business letters to major studios, independent production companies, and agents. I discovered that these people would be the audience that would best benefit from my services. That's the entire essence of selling to your buyer—presenting the features of your product or service to them and telling them how they will benefit from those products or services. Just like a good film's effect on an audience, when you're marketing your script, you should appeal to your prospective buyer's emotions in your communications to him or her.

Market Research Aids

Many resources can help you with market research, including:

- *Variety* and *The Hollywood Reporter*, called "the trades" by industry insiders. The trades are film industry publications that will tell you what scripts are being bought and which scripts are in development. In addition, the trades will tell you what elements are attached to each project.
- Hollywoodlitsales.com.
- Scriptsales.com.
- *Hollywood Creative Directory*, *Hollywood Representation Directory*, and *Hollywood Distributors Directory* contain contact information for the respective titles.
- Screenwriting craft magazines specialize in all aspects of screenwriting, including the creative and business sides. Look for magazines such as *Hollywood Scriptwriter*, *Scr(i)pt*, and *Creative Screenwriting*, the latter of which contains "The Business of Screenwriting," a business-specific column.

You may want to invest in your screenwriting career by taking a screenwriting business course, which will comprehensively teach you the business of the industry, including markets and packaging. When I took a screenwriting business course from Victoria Wisdom at UCLA Extension, I learned the importance of educating myself about the ins and outs of the film industry, about studios, producers, and production companies.

After you have researched the market, assess your script's commercial potential and packaging elements to see if they match what companies may be interested in buying. Ask yourself these questions and answer them based on your research:

1. In what way(s) is my writing and script different from the potential buyer's already produced films?
2. In what way(s) is my writing and script similar?
3. What actors and actresses can I see filling my script's character roles (protagonist, antagonist, supporting)?
4. What directors may be interested or best suited to direct my script's specific style?

PART IV

Sterilized Tools for Stitching Your Script Back Up

CHAPTER 10

The End

"The End. Is just the beginning."
—Writer's Guild of America

NOTICE THAT THE END OF THIS BOOK parallels the end of a great screenplay. A great screenplay ends mirroring some aspect of its beginning—bringing it full circle. As I stated in the beginning of this book, while you are writing a screenplay, you shouldn't concern yourself with revision and English mechanics. During the writing, you should let ideas flow freely without worrying about the finished product. In fact, that's the way you are supposed to write, creatively. Even as you refined significant areas of your screenplay, there was no need to worry about copyediting. However, now that you have completed your revision, it's time to worry about your screenplay's technical presentation. This chapter will walk you through proper script formatting, the copyediting process, including repair of grammatical and typographical errors, and protecting your baby. It's time to perfect your screenplay before submitting it to a very competitive marketplace so that it isn't rejected by its first reader.

Despite all of the time and effort you invested so far—buying this book, learning the tricks of a professional script analyst, and refining your script—all of this will not help you sell your script if it is improperly formatted. Your goal for your script, which you have written and rewritten, is to have it read by agents, producers, directors, executives, and other professionals who have the power to put your script into production.

Proper script formatting serves many purposes, including maintenance of the story's pace, and it helps with estimating a production schedule. In addition, proper formatting catches and retains the interest of industry professionals, with their notoriously deficient attention spans, and meets the production rewrite demands.

Proper Spec Script Format

In the film industry, there are two types of scripts, the spec script and the shooting script. As previously mentioned, the spec screenplay is written on the speculation that it will be sold to a studio or production company. Shooting scripts, on the other hand, are what your spec screenplay is converted to once it is bought and put into production. Spec scripts, written in a creative and descriptive style, differ from shooting scripts, which contain a lot of technical information and direction for smooth production.

As you may have guessed, the screenplay format you need to concern yourself with is the spec format. Although a spec script incorporates some shooting-script techniques and terms, some shooting script information is always omitted. These omissions are:

- *The director's rights and responsibilities.* This includes leaving camera angles and directions for the actors and actresses out of the script, which are up to the director and cinematographer to determine. The only exceptions typically include the establishment of where the shot is located (INT. or EXT.) within the scene heading.
- *The omission of music.* Unless it is relevant to the plot, leave the song choices and the score to the music director.
- *The omission of scene numbers.* Do not include scene numbers in a spec screenplay. Scene numbers will be added when the script goes into production and officially becomes a shooting script.

While some studios and production companies may have their own specific guidelines concerning typeface, binding, and margins, these are standard protocol:

- *Typeface.* Type screenplays using black ink and 12-point Courier or Courier New font. Print the document on 8¹/₂ x 11 white paper—no color other than white. This is not only because any other color looks unprofessional (you wouldn't submit a résumé on colored paper unless you're Elle Woods), but also because any revised page of a script in production is always strategically printed on different colored paper—blue, pink, green, yellow, goldenrod, and salmon respectively. This color-coding system helps the production cast and crew to locate revisions in the script and to determine when they have occurred. When I worked at the Independent Feature Project, there were stacks of multicolored paper next to the photocopier, all for use during different stages of script revision. The system greatly helps the production process.
- *Binding.* Screenplays should be three-hole punched and bound together with 1¹/₄-inch brass brads. The brads should be placed in the first and third holes of the paper only.
- *Cover and back page.* The cover and back page should be a solid color stock paper. There should be absolutely nothing written on any side of either page. I prefer to use manila for my front and back color, because it is a not-too-bold solid color.
- *Margins.* The left margin (starting from the very left edge of the 8¹/₂ x 11 paper) should be 1¹/₂ inches. Scene headings, action, and transitions should start at 1¹/₂ inches. The top and bottom of the page are both one inch, along with the right margin. Do not justify the right margin. Dialogue should be 2¹/₂ inches from the left margin, character cues are 3⁷/₁₀ inches from the left, and parentheticals (or actors' instructions) are 3¹/₁₀ inches from the left.

Buying script-formatting software is well worth the investment. With formatting software, you don't need to worry about setting margins—the program does it for you. I use Movie Magic Screenwriter and I am very pleased with it.

Now that we've covered the basics of spec screenplay format, let's dive into the nitty-gritty of screenplay format, starting with the title page.

Title Page Format

The title page of the script comes immediately after the blank cover page and immediately before the first actual page of the script. For an example of a properly formatted title page, see figure 10.1.

The title of the screenplay should appear first on the title page. Space down ten lines from the top of the page to the title. Every letter of the title should appear in capital letters. In addition, the title should be centered on the page.

Double-space, then type "by" in lowercase letters. Double-space again and type your name. If you co-wrote the screenplay, be sure to add the name of the co-author.

Now, space down about another twenty to twenty-five lines and insert your personal information, on the right or left side. On the title page of my screenplays, I always put my personal contact information on the lower left side, because the typical reading pattern is in the form of a "Z." You don't want your contact information to go overlooked. Whichever side you choose, the information should be placed at the bottom of the title page. Your personal contact information should include your name, address, phone number, and e-mail address. If you have an agent, your agent's contact information replaces your information.

It is optional to include a Writer's Guild of America registration number and/or copyright information. I typically advise my clients to omit copyright or registration information on their scripts because it is amateurish and smacks of paranoia. Copyright information also dates a script, possibly making it seem like a story that isn't good enough to sell. If you decide to include registration or copyright information, type it opposite your personal information.

TITLE PAGE

By

Your Name

Your Name
Address
Phone
Email

Figure 10.1

Story Pages Format

If you are like me, you may have trouble finding a clear, non-confusing description of the proper script format. Some guides are better than others, particularly those that incorporate a sample script with a number or letter next to each one of the components on the page that corresponds to the explanation or description of the component. However, the problem with this way of teaching format is that the writer is constantly toggling between pages—looking up the definition, then looking back to the component. I too use a sample script to teach proper format. What is different about my method is that I incorporate the definitions right into the script where the corresponding element would be, eliminating any toggling. Let's take a look at the proper screenplay format for your story pages.

The following are techniques and elements that may be incorporated within the basic but crucial format of figure 10.2.

- *Insert.* An insert (or cutaway) is used to draw the audience's attention to a particular item, such as a letter, a sign, or a newspaper. The margins for an insert are the same as scene headings, shots, and actions (1½ inches from the left). However, the content of the insert is margined like dialogue (2½ inches from the left). Once the insert is no longer needed, bring the reader back to the scene by typing (all in caps) "BACK TO SCENE," 1½ inches from the left.
- *Montage/flashback/dream sequence.* You learned about these and how to refine them in chapter 7, but now you must properly place them into your script's format. Type "MONTAGE" in all caps, followed by a single dash and then the description. An example of a montage scene heading might look like this:

MONTAGE – DESCRIPTION

FADE IN:

The Establishing Shot is typed here, double-spaced down from FADE IN and is 1.5 inches from the left margin. The Establishing Shot helps orientate the audience as to where the story is taking place. Be descriptive versus technical.

INT. MASTER SCENE HEADING-DAY

Here, following the Master Scene Heading above (which states the location of the camera and scene, and the time of day), is the action taking place within the scene. Scene headings and action are both 1.5 inches from the left margin. It is in the action that characters are introduced. If it is the first time a character makes an appearance, the name of the character must be typed in CAPS. In addition, you may want to mention some character-istics of the character. If the action is the last item on the page, roll it over to the following page. Your action may look something like this:

JENNIFER, mid-twenties and wired, punches the keys of the computer vigorously. She reveals that action is written in present tense in order to create vivid imagery for the reader.

                    JENNIFER
     The character speaking is indicated in the
     character cue. The character name stated in
     the character cue will remain the same
     throughout the entire script. The character
     cue is 3.7 inches from the left margin.

Jennifer breaks from typing and evaluates her work.

                    JENNIFER
     Everything written underneath the character
     cue is the character's actual dialogue.

Jennifer takes a sip of much needed coffee.

Figure 10.2

```
                          JENNIFER
        Dialogue is typed 2.5 inches from the left
        margin.

      Jennifer sits back in her chair, satisfied that
      she has taught all of the crucial elements of
      proper script format. But she remembers something!
      Jennifer perches in her chair and begins to type
      again.

                                              FADE OUT:
```

Figure 10.2 continued

Double-spaced from the montage scene heading, list the location of the action and then the actual action itself. It will look something like this in proper format:

Location – Action
Location 2 – Action
Location 3 – Action
Location 4 – Action

Flashbacks and dream sequences are formatted similarly, and are indicated via scene headings. Like the master scene heading, you will indicate whether the camera shot is interior or exterior, followed by the location and the time of day. In addition, you will add the word "flashback." The format will look something like this:

INT. LOCATION – NIGHT – FLASHBACK

A much more detailed description of what is happening in the flashback or dream follows the flashback and dream-sequence scene heading. Be aware that flashbacks and dream sequences should be written in present tense. The margins are the same as for scene headings and action paragraphs. When the flashback or dream sequence is finished, indicate the conclusion by typing (in caps) "BACK TO PRESENT."

- *Off Screen (OS).* "Off screen" is a term used for a character who is in the current scene but will not be seen on camera. To indicate a character who is speaking off screen, simply put the letters (all caps) "OS" on the right side of the name in the character cue.
- *Parentheticals.* Parentheticals are actors' instructions, often used to present the suggested subtext. To avoid directing the actors and actresses, use parentheticals sparingly. The margin for parentheticals is 3 inches from the left margin and every letter is lowercase. Parentheticals should be placed beneath the character cue.
- *Voice-over.* A voice-over indicates a character's inner thoughts. When a character narrates the story, this is a voice-over. To indicate a voice-over, type "VO" in capital letters on the right, next to the name of the character.

Copyediting

Once you have finished properly formatting your script, go ahead and search for grammatical and typographical errors. Figure 10.3 contains helpful tools to ensure a smooth and thorough copyediting.

Protecting Your Screenplay

You've written your screenplay. You've analyzed it. You've refined it. Formatted it. Edited it. Now is the time to protect it from unauthorized use. There are two ways to protect your script. You can register it through the Writer's Guild of America or copyright it through the U.S. Copyright Office.

The Writer's Guild of America (WGA) is a professional association consisting of television, radio, and film writers. It's a union that represents the rights of screenwriters over such issues

SYMBOL	PURPOSE	EXAMPLE OF USE	CORRECTED
ℓ	Omit	depending on it's genre	depending on its genre
(ℓ)	Omit and close	Although…	Although
( )	Close	in to the West	into the West
⟨	Insert	Profesional	Professional
⊙	Period insert	PhD	Ph.D
⟨	Comma insert	However the	However, the
≡⟨	Hyphen insert	7 ½ 8 ½	7 ½ - 8 ½
#	Space insert	Havepassion	Have passion
/	Use lowercase	Be Suspicious	Be suspicious
≡	Use capital letter	Star wars	Star Wars
⟩	Transpose	analysis	analysis

as maintenance and improvement of wages. You need not join WGA, however, to register your screenplay.

While registration of your screenplay does not protect your story title, it will protect the actual script itself, the synopsis, the treatment, and the outline.

Currently, protection is for five years, and you can renew the registration at the end five years. Registering your screenplay or related materials is extremely convenient. The WGA allows you to register via Internet, by mail, or in person. To learn more about the specific guidelines for registering your materials, contact:

Writer's Guild of America
7000 W. Third St.
Los Angeles, CA 90048

(323) 782-4500
www.wga.org

Protecting your screenplay with the U.S. Copyright Office is a more formal process, and costs change frequently. To learn more about how to copyright your material(s), visit the U.S. Copyright Office website: www.copyright.gov.

Glossary of Common Screenplay Terminology

ABOVE-THE-LINE. Refers to the creative talent on a film project. The creative talent includes actors, actresses, writers, directors, and producers.

ACT. The division of a dramatic story. A screenplay is composed of three acts.

ACTION. What happens within the plot to move the story forward.

ACT BREAK. The place (determined by plot points) where one act ends and another begins. An act break should be a seamless but conscious transition for the audience.

ANTAGONIST. The physical, mental, or emotional presence generating resistance for the protagonist during the pursuit of his or her goal.

ANTI-HERO. Very popular in contemporary cinema, the anti-hero is a protagonist who is flawed emotionally, mentally, morally, and so on.

BACK-STORY. Everything that happened to a character before the present story begins.

BEAT. An event in the story plot.

BEAT SHEET. An outline or listing of the consecutive beats (or events) that occur within the script.

BELOW-THE-LINE. Refers to the production talent of a movie project. The production talent includes editors, cinematographers, production managers, and more.

BIDDING WAR. When two or more buyers want and bid on the same screenplay.

CHARACTERISTIC. The external attributes of a character.

CHARACTERIZATION. The internal attributes of a character.

CHARACTER ARC. The mental metamorphosis of the character from the beginning of the story to the end. Some characters have no character arc.

CHARACTER-DRIVEN STORY. A story in forward motion because of the internal conflicts and challenges of the characters caused by the antagonist, physical or non-physical.

CLIMAX. Climax is the most intense plot point in a screenplay's structure. The climax occurs in act three and is followed by the resolution and denouement.

CONCEPT. The central story of a script.

CONFLICT. Caused by the story obstacles, conflict makes achieving the goal difficult for the protagonist.

COVERAGE. Story analysis and subjective comments provided by a story analyst about a screenplay.

CRISIS. The low point or second turning point in plot structure. It is the point where all seems lost for the protagonist.

DENOUEMENT. Follows the resolution in act three. It is the last plot point and is the point where any loose ends of the plot and subplot are tied up.

DEUS EX MACHINA. Literally, "god out of the machine." Used to describe a contrived ending.

DIALOGUE. Any and all of the words spoken by a character to another character(s), inevitably advancing the plot.

ELEMENTS. The creative talent, such as actors, actresses, writers, and directors, attached to a film project.

EXPOSITION. All of the information necessary for the audience to completely engage with and understand the story and characters.

GREEN LIGHT. A script that gets the green light has been given the go-ahead for production.

HIGH CONCEPT. A simplistic, blatant story idea that is aggressive and commercial.

HOOK. A scene early in the script that immediately appeals to the audience, captures their attention, and creates anticipation and interest for the events to come in the story.

INCITING INCIDENT. The point where the character's normal life is interrupted by some issue, it poses the question for the remainder of the story: whether or not the plot and/or character issue will be resolved.

INDEPENDENT PRODUCTION COMPANY. A production company with no studio deal that produces low-budget films.

LOGLINE. A basic one-line description of a screenplay's plot. The description is similar to what you may find in *TV Guide*.

LOW CONCEPT. Stories that deal with complicated subjects and are often plotted systematically and morally.

MIDPOINT. The turning point that occurs about halfway through the script. The midpoint is also where the story's action and conflict intensifies toward the climax.

MONTAGE. A series of short shots used to pass time quickly while imparting vital information to the audience with little or no dialogue.

MOVIE CROSS. A method of synopsizing an original script's concept by pairing up two already similar but different movies. *The Divine Secrets of the Ya-Ya Sisterhood* meets *Silence of the Lambs* is an example of a movie-cross.

OBSTACLE. Anything physical or mental that stands in the way of the protagonist that he or she must overcome to achieve the goal.

ORIGINAL. Adding dramatic uniqueness to an already familiar story makes a screenplay original.

PACKAGE. Describes a project that includes all the elements making it ready for submission.

PLOT. The order of events in a story.

PLOT-DRIVEN STORY. A story in forward motion because of external conflicts and challenges caused by the antagonist.

PLOT POINT. Information/moment that spins the story in a different direction.

PREMISE. See CONCEPT.

PROTAGONIST. The hero, heroine, or anti-hero of a story. The protagonist is the character that the main story revolves around.

RESOLUTION. The point of the story where all challenges have been met and the goal has or has not been achieved.

SCENE. An external unit of action in the story containing its own objective, character, conflict, beginning, middle, and end.

SPEC SCRIPT. A screenplay written purely on the speculation that it will be sold, that is, a noncontracted script.

SETTING. Where the dramatic story takes place both in the screenplay and in the film.

STAKES. What is at risk for the protagonist should he or she not achieve the goal.

SUBPLOT. The story(ies) involving the supporting characters that runs parallel to but below the main plot. A subplot is a secondary story line.

SUBTEXT. The underlying meaning of what a character says.

SYNOPSIS. A brief (one- or two-page) description of your major story points and chief characters written in present tense.

THEME. The coded moral message of the story planted consciously by the screenwriter and subconsciously decoded by the audience. Theme adds to the unity of a story.

THREE-DIMENSIONAL. Refers to characters who have deep characterization and who are dynamic rather than static in the story.

THROUGH-LINE. The main storyline of the script.

TRADES. Periodicals containing information pertaining solely to the entertainment industry.

TREATMENT. Similar to a synopsis, a treatment outlines, beat by beat, the major and minor stories and characters. The length of a treatment varies, but it is usually between five and thirty pages. A treatment is written in present tense, prose style, and its main purpose is to sell, not to describe (as does the synopsis).

TWO-DIMENSIONAL. Refers to characters who are flat, lacking nuance and depth.

VIEWPOINT. The perspective through which a story is told.

WORK FOR HIRE. Output of writer contracted by a studio or production company to write or adapt material copyrighted by the contractor.

WRITERS GUILD OF AMERICA (WGA). Professional association consisting of television, radio, and film writers. Those who join in states west of the Mississippi belong to the WGA-West (headquartered in Los Angeles). Those who join in states east of the Mississippi belong to the WGA-East (headquartered in New York City).

Bibliography

Blacker, Irwin R. *The Elements of Screenwriting*. New York: MacMillan Publishing Company, 1996.

Egri, Lajos. *Art of Dramatic Writing: Its Basis in the Creative Interpretation of Human Motives*. New York: Simon and Schuster, Inc., 1946.

Howard, David and Edward Mabley. *The Tools of Screenwriting: A Writer's Guide to the Craft and Elements of a Screenplay*. New York: St. Martin's Griffin, 1993.

Isaacs, Neil D. and Rose A. Zimbardo. *Understanding* The Lord of the Rings: *The Best of Tolkien Criticism*. New York: Houghton Mifflin, 2004.

Rosenwater, Jill Stephen and David. *Writing Analytically*. 2nd ed. Ft. Worth, TX: Harcourt, 2000.

Ruggiero, Vincent Ryan. *The Art of Thinking: A Guide to Critical and Creative Thought*. New York: Longman, 2003.

Stanton, Michael N. *Hobbits, Elves, and Wizards: Exploring the Wonders and Worlds of J.R.R. Tolkien's* The Lord of the Rings. New York: Palgrave Macmillan, 2002.

Star Wars Deleted Scenes. *Star Wars: Episode II: Attack of the Clones.* Dir. George Lucas. Twentieth Century Fox, 2002.

Trottier, David. *The Screenwriter's Bible.* Beverly Hills: Silman-James Press, 1994.

CPSIA information can be obtained
at www.ICGtesting.com
Printed in the USA
FSOW02n1944310516
21021FS

9 780826 417473